At the end of the day

At the end of the day

Church of England perspectives on end of life issues

Mia Hilborn
Brendan McCarthy
James Newcome
Mike Hill

 CHURCH HOUSE
PUBLISHING

Church House Publishing
Church House
Great Smith Street
London SW1P 3AZ

ISBN 978-0-7151-4453-4

Published 2014 by Church House Publishing
Copyright © The Archbishops' Council 2014

With the exception of the Appendices, the opinions expressed in
this book are those of the authors and do not necessarily reflect the
official policy of the General Synod or The Archbishops' Council of
the Church of England.

Typeset by Regent Typesetting, London
Printed and bound in England by
Ashford Colour Press, Gosport, Hants

Contents

Foreword

By the Archbishop of Canterbury

In the first chapter of his Gospel, St Mark tells us how a man with leprosy came to Jesus. Kneeling, this man begged him, saying: 'If you choose, you can make me clean.' St Mark tells us that Jesus was moved with pity and stretching out his hand he touched the leper, and said to him, 'I do choose. Be made clean!' (Mark 1.40–42, NRSV). With that the man was healed of his leprosy, a disease quite possibly painful and disfiguring and which would have made it impossible for him to live a normal life because it would have excluded him from his community. Jesus restored the man not just to health, but to life.

How we think about the end of our lives inevitably reflects what we think it means to be alive in the first place. Jesus' decision to care for the leper – and his action to heal him and to bring him back into community – encapsulate much of the Christian view of life that then shapes our response to the issues we can face at the end of our lives. How we care for one another, how we share one another's lives, how we live as a community that loves both the weak and the strong as made in God's image, these are actions that shape a good life and a good death.

The deaths of those we love are heightened times. The usual patterns of how we care for one another can be called into question by the pressures we face. Choosing the right thing to do becomes harder than ever when it may be the last chance we have to do right by this particular person. This book draws together the wisdom and the experience of its authors and helps us reconnect the closing stages of our lives with the whole life that we are, even then, still living. It reconnects our experience of dying with the presence of the people we share our lives with, reminding us that our living and our dying can be blessed by the care we give to and receive from others, or marred by its absence.

The advances made in medicine have transformed the lives of countless thousands of people. Yet they do not take away the need to make peace with the reality that our earthly lives will come to an end. I am therefore very grateful to the authors of this book for the contribution it will make to the conversations we have within the Church and beyond, as we seek to show Christ's own compassion in the care we give and receive 'at the end of the day'.

+*Justin Cantuar:*

About the authors

Mia Hilborn is Head of Spiritual Healthcare and Chaplaincy Team Leader at Guy's and St Thomas' NHS Foundation Trust. She is also Chair of the Chaplaincy Leadership Forum, the body responsible for representing healthcare chaplaincy to NHS England.

Mike Hill is the Bishop of Bristol. Between 2010 and 2013 he was the lead bishop for medical ethics and healthcare issues in the House of Lords.

Brendan McCarthy is the Church of England's national adviser on medical ethics and health and social care policy, working as part of the Mission and Public Affairs department of the Archbishops' Council.

James Newcome is the Bishop of Carlisle, and from 2010 the Church of England's lead bishop for healthcare issues. Since November 2013 he has also been the lead bishop for medical ethics and healthcare issues in the House of Lords.

Preface

Ethical, pastoral and practical issues associated with the end of life have been present for as long as human beings have been able to think, love and communicate with one another. So too have differing views on what constitutes 'a good death'.

Within the Christian Church many end of life issues were relatively settled for most of its history. The expansion of scientific, medical and philosophical interest, knowledge and expertise over the past few centuries, however, has laid to rest many former certainties. In particular since the middle of the twentieth century, medical advances have at first outstripped and then acted as a catalyst for much ethical, theological and pastoral reflection.

This short book takes a look at the Church of England's interaction with issues at the very end of life, from the perspectives of ethics and public policy. Each of its four main chapters provides a *personal* reflection by individuals closely associated with the Church's mission and ministry in this area. In examining the Church's involvement in medical ethics, in the debate on assisted suicide, in encouraging organ donation and in helping

to provide end of life care through healthcare chaplaincy, it offers an insight into some of the complexities
involved in contemporary end of life issues. It also
suggests some positive ways of addressing them.

Also included, in the Appendices, is a selection of some
key documents produced over the past few years by the
Mission and Public Affairs division of the Archbishops'
Council, as well as a timeline and glossary associated
with the debate on assisted suicide.

This volume offers both information with regard to the
Church of England's recent involvement in public policy
and practice in end of life issues and also an invitation to
reflect on the issues themselves. As such it represents a
unique resource for those members of the Church, and
others, who contribute in a variety of ways to caring for
people 'at the end of the day'.

1

The Church of England and medical ethics: Identifying an ethical framework

Brendan McCarthy

Shortly after I took up my position as the Church of England's national adviser on medical ethics and health and social care policy in 2009, I was tasked with preparing briefings on amendments brought to the Coroners and Justice Bill that sought, under certain conditions, to legalize assisted suicide. Hot on the heels of this debate the General Medical Council conducted a consultation on end of life care, and I was responsible for preparing an initial draft submission on behalf of the Church. In both cases it was a relatively simple undertaking to trace relevant policy statements made by General Synod or outlined by various boards or committees, and to weave them into the respective responses.

I was also aware, however, that I was not able readily to identify a clear ethical narrative running through the Church's various policy statements, particularly one that sought to describe the relationships between theology, ethics and public policy. That is not to say that such a narrative did not exist, but I could not easily identify a clear and consistent articulation of it; I suspected I might not have been alone in struggling with this. I began, therefore, to map out a theological and ethical 'back story' to the Church of England's policy statements on end of life (and other) issues, keeping in mind the Church's engagement with other social commentators and activists as well as with Parliament. What eventually emerged, through discussions with various individuals and groups both inside and outside the Church, was a template for engagement that I have found useful, not only in the context of end of life issues but also in a wide range of issues associated with medical ethics. I have employed it in numerous discussions, debates and consultations, and it has formed the backdrop to a number of recent contributions that the Church of England has made, at a national level, in the field of medical ethics.

There are, of course, varying Christian perspectives on medical ethics, reflecting the differing beliefs, principles and practices that undergird them. The Church of England celebrates theological and ethical diversity more than most, so it is not possible to construct a framework for 'public theology' that will gain the support of all. Indeed, since the Church encourages its members thoughtfully to explore issues for themselves and to make their own personal ethical decisions, diversity of opinion is to be expected and welcomed. While biblical and theological reflection, especially on the life and teaching of Jesus, play an important role in many individuals' decision making (and certainly in that of

General Synod and other official organs of the Church), others base decisions more loosely on a mixture of their Christian background, their personal experience and daily interaction with people and current ideas. It is not possible, therefore, to present a definitive Christian, or even Church of England, perspective on medical ethics, but it *is* possible to identify a number of commonly agreed features that contribute, consciously or subconsciously, to the perspectives many Church members hold.

Seeking to discover, and then to utilize, theological and ethical consensus ought not to be seen as an attempt to apply the lowest common denominator to any given issue; it is not an exercise in reducing the Church's position to the blandest shade of beige. Rather it is to recognize that diversity can be built on a common foundation that is both true to the Church's teaching and shared by a significant number of Christians.

At the most fundamental level of any ethical system lie *core beliefs* – in the case of the Church, about the nature and character of God and about God's relationship with creation, particularly with human beings. From these core beliefs stem *guiding principles* that promote positive ethical decision making, reflecting commitment, for example, to justice and love. These principles in turn find expression in *particular policies and practices*. The movement from core beliefs, through guiding principles to particular policies and practices holds true not only for Christians but for all individuals and groups that are ethically engaged with the world around them.

At the end of the day

It is an important feature of Christian ethics that both Christians and others can share the same guiding principles even though they may arrive at them from different starting points, from within different belief systems. For example, I do not have to be a Christian to believe that justice is an essential principle to follow in good ethical decision making. Similarly, particular practices may be agreed by people of differing religions or none – *shared core beliefs are not necessary for shared ethical action*. It is, I believe, particularly important to recognize this as it is usually at the levels of principle and practice, rather than core beliefs, that the Church contributes to social and political debates on medical ethics. A simple appeal to biblical teaching or to religious authority ought seldom, if ever, to be made in the mainstream of public debate even though, as I have noted, these will no doubt have played a part in helping the Church as a body, as well as many individual Christians, to develop the guiding principles they bring to a discussion.

A Christian contribution to ethical debates within society may be unashamedly Christian, but at the same time it will seldom seek to be *exclusively* Christian. While recognizing that key theological beliefs form the foundation on which the Church develops its guiding principles as well as its practices and policies, it is important that these principles and practices be debated in their own right, and not simply viewed as adjuncts to faith. As I noted earlier, it is often the case that the same, or similar, principles and practices emerge from varying underlying core beliefs. Most people, regardless of their theological beliefs (or lack of them), will agree, for example, that compassion ought to be at the heart of a mature and cohesive society, so the promotion of this and similar principles upheld by Christians ought not to be seen as 'forcing faith' on others or as an attempt to impose a 'Christian society' on the United Kingdom.

In principle, *in a genuinely inclusive society,* faith of whatever sort ought to be accepted as providing as valid a foundation for ethical debate as any other undergirding philosophy. It is not necessary to agree with a particular religious faith, or even to believe that religious belief is tenable, in order to accept that faith can provide a basis for careful ethical reflection and the promotion of good ethical principles. Secularism, which seeks to marginalize faith-based contributions in public debate, attempts, in effect, to impose its own particular philosophy on others. Continued Christian engagement in debates on ethics and public policy can help to highlight the narrowness of that stance. Inclusion, not secularism, is the sign of a healthy, tolerant and progressive society.

Core Christian beliefs relevant to medical ethics

Some of the Church's core theological beliefs are shared with other religions, some are distinctive to Christianity. While identifying these core beliefs is an essential undertaking in understanding the theological and ethical basis for the Church's engagement in public debates, I want to emphasize again that these beliefs do not usually form the interface between the Church and the rest of society in such debates. As outlined above, that interface is normally found at the level of the guiding ethical principles that these core beliefs undergird. Nonetheless it is important that Christians are able to identify which core beliefs are most relevant to medical ethics, both to enable them to understand better the relationships between theology, ethics and public policy and to explain, if asked, this process to interested parties. There is no question of the Church 'hiding' its theology from public scrutiny; rather it is a matter of finding the appropriate place for engagement with others in debates on public policy.

In the following paragraphs I outline very briefly the salient Christian beliefs that are most relevant for medical ethics. This is not an exhaustive list but it forms a basis for understanding the theological origins of the Church's ethical principles.

God the life-giver: the creation of the universe is a free and loving act of God, as a result of which the gift of life is given to human beings. While we share this gift with many other creatures, the Christian faith teaches that we are unique; of all the varied forms of life, we alone are made in God's image. The 'image of God' is not something that we possess; *it reflects something that we are*. This means that Christians understand human beings to have a particular status within earthly creation and that our innate dignity comes from being bearers of

God's image, enabling us to relate to God and to one another in a manner that reflects God's own being.

God as Trinity: God is a personal being, but however we might struggle to articulate our theology, God ought never to be understood as merely being a 'bigger' version of us. As the personal origin of all that is, God is unique; God is the archetypal 'person'. Our concept of what it means to be a person ought to come from an understanding of God, not the other way around. The Christian belief in the 'communal' unity of the Trinity, in which complete mutual love and knowledge are infinitely shared, indicates that relationship lies at the very centre of God. Consequently, relationship is intrinsic to the very concept of what it means to be a person.

God incarnate: in becoming one with humanity through incarnation in Jesus, God demonstrates selfless love, care and responsibility for humans. Metaphysical reflections on the nature of the incarnation are secondary to understanding its *significance*: relationally, God is with us, not apart from us. The incarnation also indicates that the physical and the spiritual are not two separate unbridgeable realms but that they are part of a continuum that reflects the reality of God. Creation is not something that exists 'separated' from God; rather at every level it is sustained and infused by God's presence.

God the redeemer: in the Christian doctrine of the atonement, variously expressed by a number of overlapping theories and illustrations, God takes personal responsibility for human beings and our attendant sinfulness. God freely offers eternal life through Jesus' identification with sinful humanity, demonstrated ultimately in his death on the cross. Grace, by which humans are freely given the gift of eternal life, is the hallmark of God's relationship with us and hence ought to be the hallmark of our relationships with one another. One aspect of the resurrection of Jesus is that it demonstrates God's desire to bring humanity to 'fulfilment'. As Oscar Wilde put it, 'Every saint has a past and every sinner has a future.'

God and justice: Jesus taught that our treatment of the poor, the oppressed and the vulnerable has a greater importance than we might often realize: as well as being significant in its own right, our treatment of the vulnerable is viewed by Jesus as our treatment of him. The themes of love and justice run throughout the Scriptures and are demonstrated powerfully in the life and teaching of Jesus. His identification with the vulnerable and the oppressed provides the backcloth for subsequent Christian social action.

God and community: as outlined above, a Trinitarian understanding of God indicates that relationship lies at the heart of what it means to be a person. Human beings seldom live in isolation from one another – we are bound together by ties of family, friendship and community. This is reflected in the New Testament concept that followers of Jesus are organically united in the Church, often described as the Body of Christ. We are joined to him and to one another in spiritual union. Individual, personal actions ought to be understood in this wider context – what we do affects others and this in turn affects us in a spiral of relational interaction.

Guiding ethical principles

The core beliefs outlined above form a theological 'reservoir' from which the Church may draw resources, enabling it to formulate ethical principles relevant to medical ethics. It is essential that this reservoir of know-ledge and reflection exists, but in discussions with government, Parliament and other bodies with regard to public policy, the contents of the reservoir will seldom become a focus for debate. I wish to underline, again, that this is not because the Church wishes to hide its theological convictions; rather in seeking to contribute to the creation of public policy it is essential that the Church finds an appropriate interface for discussion: an appropriate space in which it can make a meaning-ful contribution. That place is seldom going to be at the level of theological debate, but it will frequently be appropriate to engage others in discussion on the basis of ethical principles, based on theological beliefs. These or similar ethical principles may emerge from a variety of theological or philosophical belief-systems, from an eclectic mixture of reason, intuition and experience or from various amalgamations of all of these. The important point is that regardless of whichever foundational core beliefs individuals and groups might hold, these beliefs will find some expression in ethical principles. It is therefore possible for the Church to engage in constructive debate with all other interested parties in the fields of medical ethics and public policy without having either to promote or defend its distinctive theological beliefs.

With regard to medical ethics and public policy, I suggest that four overarching principles may usefully be distilled from the Church's theological reservoir. These form the crucial interface for debate and discussion with others. They also complement one another, displaying an order of precedence, the effects of each principle 'cascading' to succeeding principles. This is an important point to note as the principles themselves are perhaps likely to gain wider support than the concept of applying them in a particular order. The principles, *listed in order of priority*, are: affirming life; caring for the vulnerable; building a cohesive and compassionate community; respecting individual freedom.

Affirming life

This principle has often in the past been expressed in terms of 'the sanctity of life', but that phrase not only carries with it overtly religious overtones, it also fails to indicate what recognizing 'sanctity' entails. 'Affirming life' acknowledges that both 'the right to life' and subsequent legal protection of life, form the foundations not only of human rights law but also of much of our criminal code. Indeed, it goes further: to affirm life is to accept that each individual life has purpose, value and meaning, *even if some individuals doubt that for themselves.* It also entails striving to attain the highest quality of life possible for every person, regardless of the circumstances in which they may find themselves.

There are, of course, many ways of 'valuing' life and it is important to explore these if we are to understand how and why life ought to be affirmed. It is certainly part of the Christian tradition to believe that every person's life is of *intrinsic* value, although this idea has come under attack from some quarters. It is easy to see how belief in the intrinsic value of every life flows from the concept that every human being is made in the image of God. It is also possible, however, to come to the same conclusion from a different starting point. Those who wish to diminish the role that this belief plays within our society must ask themselves what the consequences would be if it were to be removed from our thinking. Much of our healthcare, as well as our law, is based on this belief. Why else, for example, do we expend time, money and energy in suicide prevention programmes or in caring for people living with dementia? In these situations the individuals concerned might be unable to view their own lives as possessing any value, but that does not stop others from doing so. Belief in the intrinsic value of life is an essential prerequisite for affirming life.

Other considerations ought also to be taken into account. An individual's view of his or her own life does matter, but this does not mean that we have to agree with them if they were to suggest that their lives are worthless. Individual autonomy is given an almost sacrosanct place in some people's thinking, but untrammelled autonomy is likely to lead not to the affirmation of life but in many cases to its negation.

Similarly, 'quality of life' can be utilized to encourage better care, but also misused to suggest that the *value* of a person's life can be measured by what others perceive them as being able to do or experience. Of course it is good for individuals to be enabled to experience as varied a life as possible, but such an instrumental view of life can degenerate into an assessment of a person's worth based on what he or she can do. Even worse, it can descend into an assessment of their worth based on their usefulness to others. Embracing belief in the intrinsic value of every human life will help to offset such thinking.

It is important that the principle of affirming life be interpreted to mean what it clearly implies and not stretched to incorporate, for example, the argument that it is life-affirming to bring someone's life deliberately to an end. It is a hotly debated topic whether or not it can ever be correct actively to end another person's life. Even in circumstances where such a course of action might be thought of as necessary (for example, in self-defence or in order to save other lives), it is disingenuous to suggest that this affirms life.

Affirming life takes precedence over other ethical principles relevant to medical ethics because it is fundamentally the most important and most basic guarantee that society can offer its members. Other principles are undergirded and set in a positive context by it.

Caring for the vulnerable

A civilized society is one that fundamentally affirms life and ensures that this and other benefits are fairly experienced by all of its members. In practice this means that particular attention must be paid to vulnerable individuals and groups. History indicates that the powerful often neglect or abuse the vulnerable unless strong and specific action is taken to protect them. Even where a society sets out to protect its vulnerable members, however, it is by no means assured that it will universally succeed. Such blights as child abuse, domestic abuse and elder abuse are still much too common, in spite of laws that seek to banish them. Any change in legislation that could potentially weaken the protection offered to vulnerable people is therefore to be resisted. This is so, even in cases where individuals might not recognize, or might even be resistant to the thought, that they are vulnerable.

Caring for the vulnerable, however, goes beyond protection; it also includes a commitment to ensuring that vulnerable people are supported, cared for and enabled to live fulfilled lives, afforded the same respect as other members of society. The issue for individuals living with dementia, for example, is not whether they can experience life as they once did but whether they can be enabled to live their lives as fully as possible in their current circumstances.

Building a cohesive and compassionate community

Relationship lies at the heart of what it means to be human, and the importance of relationship ought to be reflected in the way society is organized and ordered. It is almost impossible for anyone to act in total isolation from others – even our relatively trivial actions can have an extended effect that goes well beyond us as individuals. In the context of the life-and-death world of medical ethics, recognizing the communal implications of individual decisions and actions is particularly important.

It is undoubtedly true that the principle of concern for communal well-being has been abused by some societies. Totalitarian regimes have required an unacceptable level of individual compliance, exercising too much sway over the lives of their citizens. Such abuse of 'community' is inimical to building a cohesive and compassionate society. An individualistic 'free for all', however, will mean that the principles of affirming life and caring for the vulnerable are unlikely to be upheld throughout society. Individual autonomy and freedom are important, but these can only be pursued positively and fairly within a society that places them within a communal context. In other words, building a cohesive and compassionate society provides the best environment for individual freedom, ensuring that every individual's life is affirmed and that vulnerable people are cared for. Carefully gauged limitations on individual freedom that enable the building of a truly humane society ought to be welcomed by all as indicators of a mature civilization.

Respecting individual freedom

Within the context of building a cohesive and compassionate society in which life is affirmed and the vulnerable cared for, maximum individual freedom of choice and opportunity ought to be encouraged. It is, after all, individuals who are made in the image of God, not nations or organizations. Treating every person with respect and dignity is a corollary of recognizing the intrinsic value of every human life and is an essential part of creating a cohesive and compassionate society. Properly understood, 'the common good' and individual well-being go hand in hand. It has been much too easy for societies to marginalize, victimize and to persecute individuals and groups on the basis of sex, race, religion, age, disability, sexual orientation and a host of other characteristics, chosen by the powerful as grounds for discrimination. Wherever possible, therefore, in keeping with the principles already advocated, maximum individual freedom of choice ought to be underwritten by society to ensure that individuals are enabled to live their lives in the manner of their choosing.

From principle to practice

The principles above are, I believe, not only fully compatible with the core Christian beliefs that I identified earlier but emerge from them as essential ethical corollaries. Although this is the case, it can easily be seen that many people of other faiths or none might share them. At the very least they provide fertile ground for engagement with others active in the sphere of public policy – it is difficult to see how anyone serious about medical ethics could refuse to discuss them. Consequently they form the *practical* basis for the Church's engagement with others in a number of discussions and debates.

While the principles themselves might find widespread affirmation, the contention that they ought to be applied in the order of precedence outlined above is, I think, more controversial. In particular the suggestion that building a cohesive and compassionate society ought to be a prior consideration to respecting individual freedom will be contested by many. Nonetheless I believe there is both a logical and organic rationale behind the proposed order. Unless, in the context of medical ethics, affirming life is our first consideration, it is difficult to see what we might mean by the others. Similarly, unless we care for the vulnerable it is unclear what sort of cohesive or compassionate society we might be trying to build. Placing genuine communal interests above individual freedom is, I accept, a close call, but again, unless individual freedom is set in this context we shall be unable effectively to deal with competing individual aspirations or to curb individual excesses. Even if others disagree with the order suggested, this in itself will provide grounds for engagement.

The ethical spectrum

Principles, however valuable they might be, must find expression in practice if they are going make a difference to people's lives, and in the field of medical ethics there are many opportunities for putting theory into practice. It is not always clear, however, precisely how this might be best achieved. To apply our ethical principles as consistently as possible it is necessary not only to identify and prioritize them as outlined above, we must also see how they can best find expression in real-life policies and practices. This is by no means a simple task: in any given situation an array of ethical decisions and resulting practices might ensue. If we are to pick our way successfully through the maze of possible decisions and practices relevant to any given case, we need to discover a way of determining which choice or choices might best reflect our guiding principles.

A useful way of doing this is to apply the proposed principles with reference to a moral spectrum. This spectrum has at one end what we might term the ideal and at the other the universally reprehensible. In practice it is seldom the case that an ideal solution can be found and agreed upon by everyone and it is, happily, becoming increasingly rare that indisputably reprehensible morality is expressed through policy decisions. Most decisions and practices fall between these polar opposites.

In the context of medical ethics three intermediate points on the moral spectrum are useful in helping us to see how our principles might best be reflected in practice. To borrow terminology from the world of the social sciences, these may be described as the *normative*, the *non-normative* and the *anti-normative*. The normative indicates a decision or action that unambiguously reflects the principles under review, the non-normative indicates a decision or action that does not unambiguously reflect these principles but may still be acceptable because it does not contradict them, and the anti-normative indicates a decision or action that in effect contradicts the principles and consequently is unacceptable. The moral spectrum is a useful tool in ethical decision making across a range of topics.

To illustrate the principle of the moral spectrum we could look beyond medical ethics to another area, perhaps the field of law enforcement. For example, if the principle under review is 'killing is wrong', how might this be applied in the world of an armed police officer on patrol? Clearly, in an ideal world it would be unnecessary to have armed police officers but an ideal world does not exist. Equally it would be morally reprehensible for any police officer to use his or her weapon as a means of terrorizing citizens at will, and in a civilized society police officers are not given such freedom. In the real world a normative application of the principle 'killing is wrong' might be seen in a police officer arresting an armed thief at gunpoint, having first issued a warning. A non-normative application might be represented by a police officer shooting and killing an armed thief in self-defence after the thief first drew a gun and shot at the officer. An 'anti-normative' application would be represented by a police officer 'shooting first and asking questions afterwards'.

It is clear that engaging in medical ethics, particularly ethics associated with the end of life, is not an easy task for the Church. That task is made all the more difficult by the imperative to relate ethics to public policy. Very often there are no easy solutions, but the Church can be guided by its core beliefs, by guiding ethical principles and by its recognition of the moral spectrum. There will still be room for discussion, argument and disagreement both within the Church and between the Church and other bodies, but at the very least identifying a defensible template for engagement in public policy will assist the Church's witness and mission.

2

Physician-assisted suicide

Mike Hill

> Those among us who think we would want physician-
> assisted suicide if we were sick, should ask ourselves
> whether that is also what we would want for our lover
> or sister or child who was incurably ill. Would we want
> them to die quickly, so that they would not become
> a burden to us? If not, we need to look deeply into
> what 'success' would look like in this time of living we
> call dying. *(Dr Ira Byock, Palliative Care Specialist)*

With many others, I have struggled to find a way through
the moral maze that physician-assisted suicide (PAS)
raises. The Commission on Assisted Dying (CAD), which
was chaired by Lord Falconer, published its report on 5
January 2012 and advocated a change in the law to allow
a form of PAS for terminally ill patients, alongside a series
of safeguards. The Commission was by no means 'independent', however: all the commissioners were chosen
by Lord Falconer himself and the majority were known to
be advocates of some form of assisted suicide. The Commission was also funded by groups with an interest in
legitimizing assisted suicide (AS). Yet with the publication

of the report, alongside various high-profile cases where individuals have sought changes to the law to enable those who facilitate assisted suicide to avoid prosecution (Debbie Purdy, Tony Nicklinson), as well as various celebrity endorsements (Terry Pratchett), the issue has caught the public's attention in a way not seen before.

As a theist my starting point is that all life is a gift from God, therefore I have no right to make the kind of decisions PAS calls theists, or the law, to make. However, I have to recognize that not all theists believe this to be the case, and obviously not all people are convinced theists. For them this fundamental argument is of little interest. This is not an issue that remains purely academic for me. Our friend Laura was a special person who had given her life to nursing. She looked forward to retirement and time with her family as well as living her life of constant self-giving. Then she was diagnosed with motor-neurone disease (MND). Slowly but surely this awful disease overtook her. She would joke about taking a trip to a clinic somewhere in Switzerland, but she never really meant it.

I have to say that it was very hard to see this wonderful woman, and many like her, go through the degradation, suffering and loss of dignity MND visited upon her. Her faith was important to her, but for those who watched her suffer it was extremely difficult not to wonder whether PAS was, in the final analysis, the only humane way out. To date I have resisted the conclusion that it would have been the right kind of option for Laura, or that it will be in the future for others like her.

To come to this conclusion does, in part at least, make me feel like an accessory to human suffering at a terrible level. I still believe that a change in the law to allow this to happen would be a grave mistake and place us at the top of a very slippery slope, the implications of which we would not fully understand until it would be too late for some.

I suspect that it is the emotional response to living with the consequences of not 'putting people out of their misery' that most heavily influences public opinion. Support for a change in the law (though what that change might look like is not entirely clear) is said to run at 70% of adults in the UK, with a mere 16% opposed and 14% 'don't knows'. Interestingly, 72% of Anglicans (a greater percentage than in the general population) support a change in the law.[1] I am clearly in a minority!

It is doubtless true that this is a very difficult issue to discuss because people feel so strongly about it, one way or the other. It touches our deepest understandings of what it means to be human and how best to respect and cherish human life. It also touches our deepest fears: of suffering and pain, of loved ones dying or being disabled, of our own mortality and inability to cope with life. It touches us deeply because at heart most people want to act compassionately towards others. Whether one is for or against PAS, what constitutes the most compassionate response is very often far from clear. PAS might be one way of demonstrating compassion, but

1 YouGov poll commissioned for the Westminster Faith Debate on AS (April 2013).

that does not mean it is right. Other factors must also be taken into account.

Here are some of those factors. In my view they set a framework for my anxiety about the wisdom of pressing forward with a change in the law.

Terminology

First of all we need to be clear about what it is we are talking about. Language is slippery in this context and it can be all too easy for vague terms, bandied about, to catch popular attention and become influential in forming opinion. The CAD, for example, tended to use the more palatable-sounding term 'assisted dying' rather than 'assisted suicide', but that term has no legal definition or status. How we speak about matters of life and death is very important. And as much of this debate is founded on public opinion, the capacity of language to make various practices more or less acceptable in the eyes of the public must always be monitored. In the USA, the right-to-die organization the Hemlock Society changed its name to 'Compassion and Choices', for good reason.

So to be clear, 'euthanasia' is the act of deliberately ending a person's life to relieve suffering, and includes 'voluntary' and 'non-voluntary' euthanasia and 'active' and 'passive' euthanasia. 'Assisted dying' includes 'assisted suicide' and 'voluntary euthanasia'. Assisted suicide (AS) is about one individual participating in the ending of another's life. Physician-assisted suicide (PAS) is where the person assisting is a doctor. Assisted suicide is to be distinguished from withholding or withdrawing futile treatment by the medical profession, or from individuals choosing not to accept life-prolonging treatment, through an 'advance decision' (formerly known as an 'advance directive') or 'living will', for example.

Affirming life

At the start of this book a suggested framework was identified as a foundation on which to base an approach to difficult ethical issues, such as AS. There it was identified that at the centre of our theology lie certain core beliefs from which we get guiding principles that promote our decision making, and from which, in turn, we get our policies and practices.

One of these 'core beliefs' is the conviction that God is the life-giver. This underlies the belief that every human being is of intrinsic value, a view that is rightly identified as not restricted to those who hold a faith position. To believe that each and every human life is intrinsically valuable is to accept that every life has a purpose, a significance and meaning from its beginning to its end. Much of our law and our healthcare system are founded on this belief. Yet any proposal to legalize AS fundamentally undermines the premises of this core belief. From this core belief flows the conviction that societies should be ordered in a life-affirming way.

It is important to recognize that people are valuable just because they are people, in and of themselves. They are valuable because God has made them in his image (according to the Christian belief) and has given them the gift of life. People therefore continue to be valuable even when they do not feel themselves to be so, perhaps seeing themselves rather as 'not useful' or a 'burden', or their life as irretrievably damaged and painful. The moment we begin to place extrinsic judgements on the value of human lives (even our own), in terms of 'usefulness', 'bearableness' or 'quality of life', we stray into dangerous waters.

Those who suffer from any form of disability could be affected adversely by a change in the law on AS. Five major disability rights organizations in the UK oppose such change.[2] People live with all sorts of differing abilities, some of which are cited as reasons why one might want to end one's own life if AS were permissible: lack of independence, compromised dignity, physical limitations such as loss of speech or incontinence. We need to be very careful what message about the value of certain kinds of life our 'right to die' pronouncements send to those living with impairments of various sorts. At the end of a public lecture in Bristol Cathedral in 2005 the Revd Dr Christopher Newell, who himself lived with significant physical disability, said: 'dominant ideologies remove and limit attributes of personhood based upon

---

2 The Royal Association for Disability Rights, The National Centre for Independent Living, UK Disabled People's Council, SCOPE and 'Not Dead Yet'.

accounts of "nice" and "normal" and "natural" ... Every day we as individuals and as a society encounter norms that say, "better off dead than disabled".'

The Bishop of Carlisle, in his 2012 paper 'The Intrinsic Value of Life', wrote: 'To acquiesce in the ending of a life, actively assisting in suicide, is to state that the value of a human life may be extrinsically determined.'[3] It is, admittedly, not straightforward to argue that a person should not be allowed to take their own life with the help of another, even when it is their own wish, but the consequences of undermining belief in the absolute value of human life is to open the door to other situations in which lives may be taken for different reasons. If we do not believe that each life is valuable and ought to be protected, why prevent murder, advise against suicide, condemn infanticide or oppose capital punishment? It is never life-affirming to end the life of another.

Stanley Hauerwas and Richard Bondi set the context for opposing suicide and euthanasia: 'To end one's life, either by one's own hand or by requesting the hand of another to do it, places too great a burden on those that are left, as it asks us to co-operate in a process that we should keep distant from. To ask us passively or actively to co-operate in the ending of a life opens us to temptations best kept at bay – that we should determine for another whether they will live or die.'[4]

---

3 'The Intrinsic Value of Life', 2012, at www.churchofengland. org/media/1387055/intrinsicvalueoflife.pdf.

4 Stanley Hauerwas and Richard Bondi, 'Memory, Community and the Reason for Living: Theological and Ethical Reflections on Suicide and Euthanasia', in *JAAR* 44.3, 1976, pp. 439–52.

We do not have to look far to see how arguments used in favour of PAS can later be used to defend voluntary, and even involuntary euthanasia. Such is the case in the Netherlands, where a change in the law has slowly but surely influenced popular opinion, medical opinion and legal practice about what constitutes acceptable ending of life. In the USA, PAS is legal in the states of Oregon, Washington, Montana and Vermont. Recent statistics from Washington show an increase of 130% in instances of AS since the state's 'Death with Dignity' Act took effect.

A belief in the absolute value of every human life is a facet of belief that a society (not just the religious components of it) undermines at its peril: 'The prohibition against suicide is a way of affirming how we should die in our communities in a non-destructive way for those that continue after us. It is a symbolic claim that insists that we remember our primary business is about living, not dying.'[5]

Protecting the vulnerable

The second value Christians tend to hold as significant in arguments against AS is a fundamental concern for the vulnerable and weak and a belief in the necessity to protect and cherish those less able to care for themselves. The way we treat the vulnerable speaks of the

5 'Assisted Dying/Suicide and Voluntary Euthanasia', Church of England paper, March 2009, at www.churchofengland.org/media/57990/assisteddyingpdfmar09.pdf, 449.

way we treat Jesus himself (Matthew 25.35–46; Luke 10.25–37). But again, it is not necessary to hold a faith position to believe in the need to protect the weak and vulnerable. It is an oft-quoted tenet that any civilized society must be judged by the way it treats its weakest and most vulnerable members.

Few can be considered more vulnerable than those whom proponents of AS consider prime candidates for being helped to take their own lives. The stresses of long-standing and terminal illness are immense, and the potential pressure upon terminally ill people to consider ending their lives must not be underestimated. Indeed, 60% of people who oppose a change to the law on AS do so on the basis that 'vulnerable people could be, or feel, pressurized to die'.[6]

Those who are vulnerable in our society must also include the elderly and infirm, whose plight at the hands of those who are supposed to be caring for them has been vividly documented over the last few years. Failures in duty of care in care homes, terrible examples of 'elder abuse' and a catalogue of cases where older people have been neglected and exploited fill our screens and newspapers. A third of a million people each year suffer from 'elder abuse'. In one quarter of cases there is a financial motive. Any change in the law to legalize AS could, potentially, lead to a growing pressure on the elderly to save others from the burden of having to care for them.

6 YouGov poll commissioned for the Westminster Faith Debate on AS (April 2013).

There is evidence that where AS has been legalized, a major reason for people considering it for themselves is a fear of becoming a burden to others. Yet the Christian gospel calls us to care for our brothers and sisters, our neighbours and even our enemies, in such a way that no person should ever be seen, or consider themselves to be, burdensome to others (Galatians 6.2; Colossians 3.13; Ephesians 3.2).

The question of how we adequately protect vulnerable people from undue coercion should the law change on AS has by no means been satisfactorily answered. In an attempt to address it, the CAD put forward a series of safeguards to protect against misuse of the law. Many fear that these are not sufficiently robust to protect vulnerable people in terminal illness.

The safeguards include two doctors being required independently to confirm that a person is 'likely to die within 12 months'. Practitioners point out, however, that such a diagnosis is difficult, unreliable and unworkable. There is the additional issue of finding two doctors who are willing to offer judgement of this kind when most doctors are against PAS. It could mean, therefore, that just a small number of doctors become involved in most PAS applications, leading to questionable independence. The CAD states that a person must have a 'settled intention to die' and that there must be a cooling-off period of two weeks (the same period as for a hire-purchase car). This is woefully inadequate, given the mental, physical and emotional stress that people with terminal illness could well be feeling. It may take as long as six months to rule out a clinical diagnosis of depression, for example. The CAD talks about 'voluntariness and absence of coercion', but such vague terms will be very difficult to define or enforce. What might constitute 'undue influence', for example? The CAD recommends a statutory code to review each case for compliance. It will, of course, be too late to undo any 'mistakes'.

The issue of caring for the vulnerable with compassion is by no means straightforward. Many advocates of PAS would say that allowing someone to choose when to die and helping them to do so with dignity is the most compassionate response. However, it seems obvious to me that the very best way to show compassion for a person is to care for them. Of course PAS advocates would say that AS can be seen as a kind of care. The reasons cited by people requesting assisted dying in the US state of Oregon, where AS has been legalized, include a decreasing ability to participate in activities that made life enjoyable (90.1%), loss of autonomy (88.7%) and loss of dignity (74.6%).[7] Faced with such anguish about living with significantly reduced capacity, it can be easy to think that helping someone find a 'way out' is the most compassionate option. However, in a French survey of people who had experienced 'locked-in syndrome', most (68%) said they had never had suicidal thoughts, and 72% said they were happy.[8] What might

---

7 2011 Report of Oregon 'Death with Dignity' Act.

8 Research from the French Association for Locked-in Syndrome published in *The BMJ Open*, February 2011.

be seen as compassionate for one person might not be for another.

Compassion itself could well be fuelled and driven by a host of other factors, including deep-rooted fears about what might happen if we or our loved ones were faced with similarly intractable circumstances. Palliative care specialists, who are concerned to treat the whole person, are distrustful of legislation, seemingly in the name of compassion, that is founded on fear of suffering: 'These sorts of fears are leading people to ask whether there is a place for physician-assisted suicide (PAS). At first sight this call appears to be driven by compassion for the individual and to be a way of respecting their rights. However, making facilities available to help someone kill themselves may be more likely to reduce the respect that we have for human life in general and is not the most appropriate way of helping that person.'[9]

It is estimated that on average 30 people a year die in the UK as a result of AS, but there have been no prosecutions since the Director for Public Prosecutions introduced relevant guidelines on prosecution in cases of AS in 2010. The current legislation does not legitimize AS in any way, and continues to act as an effective deterrent for those who would use AS unscrupulously, but it does continue to allow for a compassionate response to individuals who have assisted a loved one to die when

9 Dr Kathryn Myers, consultant in palliative medicine at Mildmay Hospital, writing in 2000 in *Christian Medical Fellowship Files*, no. 9, cited in GS1851A, Church of England General Synod, Private Member's Motion, 'Independent Commission on Assisted Dying', January 2012.

they have acted out of compassion and without any hope of personal gain. Baroness Findlay of Llandaff has called it 'a law with a stern face and a kind heart'.[10] As the Bishop of Swindon said about AS in a newspaper article responding to the publication of the guidelines, 'If we want to build a society which majors on compassion and care, which supports those who are dying or fearful of growing infirm and a burden, there are far better roads for us to travel [than AS].'[11]

Any change in legislation that could weaken protection for the vulnerable is to be resisted. Brendan McCarthy, in his paper on the CAD report, sums it up well when he says: 'Current legislation protects vulnerable people from being encouraged to commit suicide, from being pressured to do so and from feeling that it is a matter of indifference to society if they live or die.'[12]

Living together

Arguments for AS often centre on the concept of the individual's 'right' to choose when to die and in what manner. Of those who support a change to the law,

10 Baroness Findlay of Llandaff, Professor of Palliative Medicine at Cardiff University and Chairwoman of the All Party Parliamentary Group on Dying Well, writing on 'The dangers of assisted suicide' in epolitix, March 2009, at http://centrallobby.politicshome.com/latestnews/article-detail/newsarticle/baroness-finlay-of-llandaff-the-dangers-of-assisted-suicide.

11 Lee Rayfield in *The Guardian*, Thursday 25 February 2010.

12 Brendan McCarthy, 'Turning a Blind Eye: The Falconer Commission and Assisted Suicide', at www.churchofengland.org/media/1387081/turningablindeye.pdf.

82% do so because 'an individual has the right to choose when and how to die'.[13] However, the very word 'assisted' shows that at least one other must be involved. The action of a person who takes their life always has an impact on others, whether it is the person assisting them or family, friends and wider relationships.

The biblical narrative understands people as existing in community, reflecting the nature of God himself who is three persons in one, Father, Son and Holy Spirit, and in their mutual and interdependent relating to each other. Society is not simply a collection of individuals. No one person exists in isolation from others. The communal implications of individual decisions are important and certain limitations on individual freedoms must be put in place to enable the building of a humane society. Hauerwas points out that the problem with suicide in general is that it erodes the belief that 'our very existence – that is our willingness to be present – has moral significance that we seldom notice'.[14] 'Our willingness to be present' is partly born of an allegiance to those around us, those with whom we share life and those who would be affected by our death.

The concept of 'autonomy' features prominently in the debate on AS. The very idea of autonomy is a strange concept to grapple with if one believes, as Christians do, that a network of interrelationships is the proper context

---

13 YouGov poll commissioned for the Westminster Faith Debate on AS (April 2013).

14 Hauerwas and Bondi, 'Memory, Community and the Reason for Living', p. 444.

for the flourishing of human life. Autonomy is not the same as saying a person has the right to do whatever they like, and we need to bear in mind that all our individual actions might impinge on the rights of others. One person's right to autonomy could remove the same right from others. For example, PAS is not a private act but one that could be seen to impinge on the doctor's autonomy.

A degree of limited autonomy is already recognized in the law for end of life issues, through living wills and advance decisions whereby a person is to some extent able to order the manner of their dying. But the kind of arbitrary autonomy proposed by advocates of a change in the law on AS leads to an abandonment of the concept of any intrinsic, societally protected value for human life, in favour of the protection of the right of each individual to choose the timing and method of their own death and carry out this choice in practice, with assistance from others.

What might be more helpful is a concept of 'principled autonomy' whereby we recognize that 'our actions affect others directly and indirectly and this reality ought to place boundaries on unbridled autonomy'.[15] This recognizes that what might be seen as greater freedom of choice for some will be a source of pressure for others. The balance between communal interest and individual freedom is not straightforward, but at their

---

15 'Assisted Dying/Suicide and Voluntary Euthanasia', Church of England paper, March 2009, at www.churchofengland.org/media/57990/assisteddyingpdfmar09.pdf.

best the common good and individual well-being ought to nourish and inform each other.

A major impact that any legalization of PAS is likely to have on the 'common good' relates to its possible effect on the medical profession. Changing the law on PAS could fundamentally alter the nature of the medical profession and undermine the trust currently placed in medical practitioners. The International Code of Medical Ethics states that 'A doctor must always bear in mind the obligation of preserving human life from conception.' It is hard to see how any legalization of PAS would not undermine the call to 'preserve human life'. Legalizing PAS would place a pressure on doctors to be arbiters of life and death in a manner that does not sit well with their remit to 'do no harm'. Of people who oppose a change to the law, 55% believe that 'it places too much of a burden on the person or people who help someone to die'.[16]

Were PAS to be legalized, in order for it to be universally available it would have to be administered under the auspices of the NHS. This would radically change the nature of the NHS. With pressure on its budgets always increasing, the temptation to see PAS as a 'cost-effective treatment' would be ever present. It is for these reasons, among others, that many in the medical profession are against AS. The British Medical Association declined to participate in the Commission for Assisted Dying. A change in the law is opposed by

16 YouGov poll commissioned for the Westminster Faith Debate on AS (April 2013).

95% of palliative care specialists and 65% of doctors. Most medical practitioners would prefer instead that the money and resources that would inevitably be taken up by the structures needed to support and administer the legalization of PAS should go instead towards increasing the coverage and quality of good end of life care packages across the country. Palliative care specialists know that great advances in the field have been made over recent decades, and whereas in the past people often died in distress, pain and fear, there is no reason that, given the right support and resources, this should happen to anyone today. Practitioners are keen to expand the coverage of full palliative care packages that include psychological, social, family and spiritual support to address the needs of terminally ill people.

This is a difficult issue and one that contains many conflicting emotions and reasons. The overwhelming sense I have is that the outcome of a change in the law would unleash a range of unintended consequences that we might live to regret. Our experience of the 1967 Abortion Act, for example, is far from encouraging. Legislation put in place then was intended to be prescriptive and to limit abortion to extreme risks to the health (including the mental health) of mother and/ or unborn child. Since then the legislation has, in my view, been subject to 'criteria slippage'. The fact that we are now engaged in discussions about whether or not factors such as cleft palate or Down's syndrome, or even gender, have any relevance to the criteria is surely evidence of this slippage.

Of course, in the end all this is about people and their lives and deaths, and consequently requires us to speak with great care and understanding. Caricaturing those who take an opposing view to the Church of England's official position and who favour a change to the law on assisted suicide as being insensitive or misguided, or both, is unhelpful. It is my hope that a robust debate will continue to surround these issues, and that the voices of those with a faith position will continue to be heard among the rest.

3

Organ donation

James Newcome

The transplantation of organs is nothing new. It has been suggested that grafts of one sort or another were taking place in Ancient Egypt as long ago as 3500 BC. However, the history of our 'modern' transplant techniques really begins in 1905 with corneal transplants (eyes can be removed up to 24 hours after death, and the success rate is extremely high). The first successful renal transplant (between identical twins) followed in 1954, and on 3 December 1967 a heart was transplanted at Groote Schuur Hospital in South Africa. This ushered in a whole new era of organ donation, which has now become relatively commonplace and includes not only heart and kidneys but also lungs, liver, pancreas and the small bowel (together with tissue such as corneas, skin, bone and heart valves).

Transplant surgery has also become a great deal safer over the years. In the early days of cardiac transplantation only 24 out of 154 recipients survived. But in the twenty-first century the problem is less one of survival than of supply. The statistics are startling. About 1,000 people die each year waiting for an organ (three per day), while in 2012/13, 3,113 transplants took place from 1,212 deceased donors. There are about 8,000 people in the UK on the active waiting list at any given moment, together with another 2,500 temporarily suspended from the list because they are unfit or unavailable. More than 90% of British people claim to be in favour of organ donation (and would take an organ if it were needed), but only 18.5 million (29% of the population) were on the Organ Donation Register in 2012. In fact the UK is still at the lower end of European organ donation rates, even though the Organ Donation Taskforce has made big strides towards its objective that 'donation should be a usual part of end-of-life care'.

The cost of such a large gap between supply and demand is substantial, in terms of money as well as misery. For instance, there are hundreds of people with an incurable kidney disease who could be given new life with a renal transplant but instead are being kept alive with dialysis – which remains an intensive and time-consuming resource (12–14 hours per week) and costs more on an annual basis than a kidney transplant operation. The savings over the average life of a deceased donor kidney (10.5 years) are approximately £250,000 when compared to dialysis. Despite recent advances we badly need to find more donor organs, and if anything the problem is getting worse rather than better. Hospitals are now reimbursed for retrieving organs, so at least one financial disincentive has been removed. But because the majority of people do not die under circumstances that make organ donation possible (e.g. at home, in an accident, or even on a general ward in hospital), there is a certain urgency about making sure that when it can happen, it does.

Of course that doesn't mean ignoring the many legal, ethical, medical, social and economic issues raised by organ donation. Just because we can do something we cannot automatically assume it should be done; and although transplant surgery is now so well established, it continues to pose a number of difficult questions. I intend to cluster these under nine headings, with an eye on the four 'guiding principles' set out at the beginning of this book (affirming life; caring for the vulnerable; building a cohesive and compassionate community; respecting individual freedom).

Defining 'death'

By what criteria can we determine when someone is actually 'dead'? This has obvious implications for the removal of organs from a 'deceased' donor, and it has become a great deal more complicated now that machines can keep people's bodily functions (such as heartbeat and breathing) going almost indefinitely. Advances in medical knowledge and technology have, ironically, made it much more difficult to define death now that the traditional definition (the 'permanent cessation of spontaneous heartbeat and breathing') no longer applies. Some would say that we can't properly define anything when we don't fully understand its meaning. But what is absolutely clear is that our definition of death is heavily dependent on our definition of what it means to be human (cf. the 'guiding principles'). If we regard human beings simply as machines or collections of 'physiological signs of life', then we will always be tempted either to prolong these signs as long as possible by artificial means or to redefine death in such a way as to harvest more organs for transplant. The need for an organ should never be the cause of declaring a donor to be 'dead', which is one reason why new guidelines for 'diagnosing death' were produced in 2008. Also, the 'deceased donor rule' makes it clear that the process of organ retrieval must not be the cause of the donor's death.

There are four 'stages' in the process of dying, which are usually described as clinical death (when the 'vital functions' of heart and breathing cease), brain death, biological death and cellular death.

Clinical death, the first stage, can sometimes be restored (e.g. after drowning) by artificial resuscitation and cardiac massage; and a ventilator can give the impression that someone is still very much alive, even when brain death (caused by lack of oxygen, which means that the brain ceases to function) leads to biological death (loss of organ function). After massive brain damage, the 'reversal' of clinical death does not necessarily mean the restoration of any 'life' as we might understand it. What is more, the final stage – cellular death – starts to happen at a different rate for different cells.

In the 2008 document referred to above it is proposed that for clinical purposes there is only one type of death,

namely a state in which an individual has permanent-
ly and irreversibly lost the capacity for consciousness
and the ability to breathe unaided (both of which are
functions of the brain). It goes on to argue that this state
can be arrived at in different ways and that dependent
upon the precise mechanism, different criteria for how
it is recognized should apply. Most commonly, death
occurs after loss of the function of the heart (e.g. following a heart attack), brain function (the essence of death)
being the result of the failure of its supply of oxygen
that follows. Death is diagnosed by confirming that the
heart has stopped beating and that the patient is totally
unresponsive and not breathing. Less commonly, death
follows direct injury to the brain, for instance following trauma to the head or a brain haemorrhage. If no
medical attention is to hand then breathing ceases and
soon after the heart, and while the sequence of events
is different, the various features are the same. However,
if the patient is promptly resuscitated at the time of the
brain injury, the heart continues to beat because the
lungs are ventilated with a supply of oxygen. This is the
state of brain-stem death.

The current ethical debate has focused largely around
'brain-stem death' and what that really means. In a
letter to the *Church Times*, in response to an appeal by
the Church of England for more organ donors in 2011,
Drs David Evans and Michael Banner objected that 'the
scientific basis for the claim that brain-stem death ensures
there can never again be any form of consciousness is in-
secure'. They saw this definition as 'a reductionist version

of brain death' and insisted that potential donors should be informed that their heart and lungs would be kept going artificially while organs are removed. They also pointed out that some theatre registers 'record the time of death of the donor as the time when the ventilator was turned off at the end of the procedure'.

But it has to be said that this is not the view of a majority of medical practitioners, who regard death as 'a process event rather than a momentary event'. Some of our systems can remain alive while others have died – which is why it is so important to define death 'appropriately' for different circumstances. Most practitioners do believe that the current definitions of death (and their associated tests) as they apply to organ donation are entirely appropriate – and those definitions are available to 'prospective donors, relatives and all interested parties'. In its guidelines the BMA is quite clear that when brain-stem tests have been completed the patient is actually 'dead', whether or not heart and lung function is being maintained on a ventilator. In fact brain-stem death is 'the clearest manifestation of death rather than some special form of death' – and it is hard to see any moral objection to keeping a person's heart and lungs going artificially in order to preserve internal organs once the central nervous system has broken down. When the tests have been correctly performed, no patient who has been declared dead has ever recovered any element of brain function.

Brain-stem death is now generally accepted as the main criterion for the 'irreversible destruction of the brain', and it is emphatically not the same as a 'persistent vegetative state', in which primitive functions of the brain stem, including respiration, are preserved. A patient in a persistent vegetative state breathes for themselves and is not dependent on a mechanical ventilator. Continuing physiological 'existence' is not the same as 'human life', and someone who is 'brain dead' is not really alive in any human sense since our capacity for reason and abstract thought is something that distinguishes us from other forms of life. Before brain-stem death it is possible to be legally and medically alive even though insensible; but after brain-stem death, without artificial help all life ceases. There is no response to internal or external stimuli, and it involves a complete loss of both higher and lower brain functions. In other words, death is a 'demonstrable fact'.

From this the crucial importance of various 'end of life care protocols' can be appreciated. These largely revolve around potential conflicts of interest between the dying donor and the potential recipient of his or her organ. So, for instance, the doctors who declare someone dead should be quite separate from the transplant team. What is more, 'early withdrawal of treatment' should only happen if it has been validly requested by the patient or, more usually, the patient's family, and should always be in the patient's best interests. Equally there may be occasions when the patient gives permission for treatment to be prolonged beyond the point where it is medically beneficial in order to benefit others through organ donation. Sometimes this can be psychologically – if not physically – beneficial. So in 2011 the UK Donation Ethics Committee declared that when someone wants to be a donor, after 'circulatory' death 'it is ethically acceptable to take steps to facilitate, or at least not to frustrate the patient's wish to donate organs after death provided the steps are not contrary to the patient's interests'. The patient's best interests are as central to end of life care as to all care (cf. the Hippocratic Oath).

Choice of recipients

The BMA is quite clear that the main medical criterion for receiving a donated organ should be 'critical need'. Apart from dialysis, the recipient should have no hope of longer-term survival without a transplant – though of course the patient does need to be well enough to survive the necessary surgery, and this can involve hard decisions about whether or not there is any point going down that road.

Questions also have to be asked about future quality of life. Respect for each human being's well-being and individual freedom means that it may not always be appropriate simply to 'prolong a life' – which is not, anyway, the ultimate purpose of medicine. As Catherine Lyons puts it, 'The fact that life is being prolonged does not necessarily imply that life has been saved.' Any surgical procedure should enhance the patient's life rather than demoralize him or her. For example, a heart transplant should aim at 'the long-term restoration of a critically ill patient to a productive and personally enjoyable life'.[1] The difficulty comes in knowing whether or not that will be the case – and when there are not enough organs to go around, how do you choose between several patients who are all in 'critical need'?

One solution that has been proposed to this dilemma is so-called 'reciprocity'. This would entail people who are on the Organ Donor Register receiving preferential treatment if and when they are themselves in need of a transplant. Both the NHS and the Church are fundamentally opposed to this idea, arguing that treatment should be according to need, not merit; and both stress the importance of the 'gift relationship' involved in organ donation. Surveys admittedly suggest that the prospect of priority access can act as a considerable inducement to donation. But organs must be donated 'freely and voluntarily' and reciprocity represents a clear breach of the 'clinical need' principle. It is also the thin end of a fairly large wedge of other social and economic factors.

These include the donor specifying who should receive his or her organs. That remains permissible for living donors (e.g. donating a kidney to a family member) but not usually for 'cadaverous donation'. In 1998 a donor's family stipulated that a particular organ should only go to a white recipient, but the BMA was then – and remains – utterly opposed to 'conditional donation'. As

---

1 Catherine Lyons, *Organ Transplants: The Moral Issues*, London, SCM Press, 1970, p. 18.

well as being donated freely and voluntarily, organs must be offered unconditionally, so specifying in advance a particular ethnic or religious group is not acceptable. When the organ has been removed from a deceased person it belongs to the community, and it is for the community to decide on an appropriate recipient.

Of course, that simple statement in itself begs a number of questions. Should the age of the recipient be taken into account? What about the tissue-typing and relative chances of success? It makes *economic* sense to prioritize people who are utilizing scarce resources (e.g. dialysis), can afford to pay (private patients) or are thought of as being 'of most value' to the community. But economic arguments are not necessarily the most ethical – and at present they play no part in the selection of recipients, though when the cost and use of resources in an increasingly hard-pressed NHS is discussed, some would question the justification for heart transplants as against hip replacements and other less expensive surgery.

Experimentation

Without experimentation, organ transplants would not have become as commonplace or as successful as they now are. But experimentation itself poses a dilemma, expressed very well in the early days of developing transplantation techniques by Samuel Stumpf: 'The dilemma we face is how to achieve two highly desirable goals, namely, the expansion of medical knowledge and the protection of the dignity and security of the individual.'[2] The question is how far you can use a person to gain medical knowledge before it becomes misuse or even abuse. If the relationship of trust that is so important between doctor and patient is not to be irreparably damaged, the patient needs to be extremely well informed about the nature – and possible effect – of the experiment. He or she also needs to be capable of making a reasonable response.

Fundamental to this debate is the need to treat people as ends in themselves rather than the means to an end. As Immanuel Kant observed, they must be regarded as persons – not objects or simply subjects for experimentation. The 'permissible limits' of experimentation therefore need to be determined more by the potential benefit of the transplant than by the possible long-term by-products of the procedure.

That has particular repercussions for the use of immunosuppressive drugs. Huge advances have been made in their effectiveness, but while they are excellent for avoiding the rejection of a donated organ it is still the case that they reduce the body's ability to fight off infection. They help the patient not to resist the 'foreign body' but at the same time make it harder to resist viruses and bacteria, and some immunosuppressants actually accelerate the spread of cancer cells. Without

---

2 Samuel Stumpf, 'Some Moral Dimensions of Medicine', in *Annals of Internal Medicine*, 64, 1966, quoted in Lyons, *Organ Transplants*, p. 27.

them, the body will keep 'intruders' out; with them, especially after a heart transplant, there is a greater danger of letting any 'intruders' in.

Organ procurement

In a report published in 2000, the BMA asked for 'more direct appeals for people to register as donors'. As it pointed out, acts of selfless generosity 'transform both the donor and the recipient', and the aptly named 'Flesh and Blood' Campaign mounted by the NHS in partnership with the Church (2012–14) has been especially successful in prompting a significant increase in the number of donors (of blood as well as organs).

However, at the time of writing a debate continues over the relative merits of an opt-in or opt-out system of organ procurement. The BMA is absolutely committed to 'opting out with safeguards', which will be the default position in Wales as from 2015. However, although a direct causal link between 'presumed consent' and a higher number of transplants (e.g. in Belgium) seems likely, it has yet to be proved, and the Church of England favours a 'hard' opt-in system, which would involve 'a rather less intrusive shift in the State's relationship with its citizens'.

At present we have what might be described as a 'soft' opt-in system in England, which tries to maintain a delicate balance between the rights of individuals, relatives and the state. Individuals can decide (within certain limits) how their bodies should be used after death. Relatives are usually consulted and their views respected, even when these contradict the wishes of the deceased. Meanwhile the state has little power to determine what should happen to someone's organs, except in very exceptional circumstances (e.g. a public health crisis). This presumes a person's right not to have his or her organs removed after death unless specific consent has been given (hence a statement by the Roman Catholic Bishops' Conference to the effect that organ donation 'is not morally acceptable if the donor or his proxy has not given explicit consent'). It also preserves the idea of organ donation as a 'conscious gift', freely given, and 'hard' opt-in would mean that signing up to the Organ Donation Register would have the same legal force as, for example, a clause in a will. 'Nudge theory' has a part to play here, and is already being employed up to a point via online applications for driving licences. This could be extended to passport applications and completed tax returns.

However, neither the BMA nor the Church favours a third option, known as mandated choice. No country has yet gone down this route, and limited evidence from Texas suggests that if people are forced to choose between saying Yes or No to organ donation, they tend to veer towards the negative. Also, as the BMA points out, compelling people to make a choice of this kind 'could be seen as undermining rather than enhancing their autonomy', while penalizing non-compliance could be seriously counterproductive.

Indeed, everyone agrees that the main aim of any 'donation campaign' should be encouraging discussion of the issue within families. When relatives are unaware of the dead person's wishes they tend to be reluctant about organ donation, whereas consent rates are much higher when the issue has been aired in a family. In fact relatives only consent in about 40% of cases when there has been no discussion, but this rises to 90% when discussion has taken place. Under our present system, 'having the conversation' is regarded as the real key to progress with regard to the availability of organs.

Some argue that when a person has joined the Organ Donor Register, 'the scruples of relatives' should not be allowed to negate his or her clear wish. Preservation of life should take precedence over matters of sentiment. But – as with the Liverpool Care Pathway – press coverage of particular incidents has not helped, and of course relatives are being asked for their opinion at an extremely difficult and emotional moment. Legally, their wishes are not meant to override the wishes of the deceased – but in practice few doctors would insist on going ahead with donation against the family's will, even though some recently bereaved relatives subsequently feel guilty about a negative response.

There is a particular issue here with regard to minority ethnic communities. These currently constitute 11% of the overall population of the UK; 28% of people on the transplant list; and only 4% of kidney donors. Among black and minority ethnic relatives, the consent rate for donation for family members who are deemed 'brain dead' is just 27% compared with 71% for Caucasian relatives. Some of the obstacles to consent include: cultural objections; confusion about the system; a reluctance to discuss death; fear of bodily disfigurement.

Other concerns in the area of organ procurement include the transplantation of animal organs and their possible psychological effects (not to mention objections by animal rights activists). Pig organs (e.g. heart valves) are most usual. Chimpanzees are immunologically closer but too expensive – and baboon organs (e.g. kidneys) don't last very long.

Then there is the interesting question of payment for organ donation. The BMA Medical Ethics Committee points to a whole series of ethical arguments around consent. Since many of those who would seek payment are 'poor and in need', there is a real possibility of coercion and exploitation; and paying someone for an organ (e.g. £28,000 for a kidney as suggested in a *British Medical Journal* article) shifts the whole basis of our system from altruism to commerce. The end (more organs) does not justify the means (which turns our bodies into commodities and undermines our concept of human dignity). So the BMA is opposed to incentives or direct payment for donation, and the EU Organs Directive specifically prohibits any payment for organs from living or dead donors. The most that can happen is the reimbursement of necessary expenses.

Nor has the suggestion made by the Nuffield Council on Bioethics that funeral costs for donors should be met been greeted with much enthusiasm. This happens in Israel and parts of Spain, but again it involves an adjustment of motivation – from altruism to the benefit of one's family.

Finally under this heading it is worth noting that more than 20% of donors are now critically obese (with a body mass index greater than 30). Ten years ago the proportion was 12%. At the same time, 30% of donors are now over 60. Together these figures translate into fewer useful organs per donor and highlight the continuing need for more people to join the Organ Donor Register.

The religious dimension

In the sixteenth century a 'tissue-grafter' at the University of Bologna called Gaspare Tagliacozzi was heavily criticized by some theologians for 'interfering with God's handiwork'. Today a few Christians continue to regard organ transplantation as cannibalization and even 'the work of the devil'; and some Pentecostals have voiced doctrinal objections based on a particular understanding of the resurrection of the body. Jehovah's Witnesses refuse even blood transfusion due to their interpretation of Leviticus 17.11–14 (though this objection can be overruled by a court when the patient is a sick child).

However, the Church of England and most other 'mainstream' Christian denominations are strongly in favour of organ donation, which is now regarded as part of our stewardship of God's gifts. To quote from a statement made in 2012 by its Department of Mission and Public Affairs, 'giving one's self and one's possessions voluntarily for the well-being of others and without compensation is a Christian duty of which organ donation is a striking example. Christians have a mandate to heal, motivated by compassion, mercy, knowledge and ability. The Christian tradition both affirms the God given value of human bodily life and the principle of putting the needs of others before one's own needs.' Bringing life out of death by offering hope in tragedy resonates very powerfully with the Christian story, and the main ethical issue for Christians is how to treat everyone justly and fairly given that we are all made in God's image. In 2013 Joanne Cox summed up this new approach in a *Church Times* article with the words, 'I no longer see donation as a charitable act: now I think of it as nothing less than a Christian duty.' She went on to say: 'our bodies are not the enemy, but the very gift of God – and it is our responsibility to celebrate and use them as we should the other gifts we have been given.' In other words, the generous and sacrificial donation of organs should be regarded as an aspect of Christian service because it helps to save and enhance the lives of others.

All the major religions of the UK support the principles of organ donation and transplantation. While one of the main reasons given by members of black and minority ethnic communities for not joining the Organ Donation Register is religion, a great deal of useful work has been done by the Department of Health with religious communities in the UK to make the positions of the different faiths clear in this respect and to encourage donation rates. It is important to note that the UK-based Muslim Law (Shariah) Council issued a ruling in 1995 allowing Muslims to carry donor cards, and that this ruling was supported by some of the most prestigious Islamic legal authorities in the world. Some Muslim scholars in the UK and more widely, however, prohibit organ donation. Difficulties include objections to any procedure that might be regarded as 'bodily mutilation', problems defining brain-stem death as 'real death', and the issue of respecting the modesty of those who are dead and dying. One of the main arguments for Muslims in favour of organ donation is the principle that 'necessities permit the prohibited' so that the benefit of saving a life outweighs the personal cost borne by the donor. As the Qur'an says, 'Whosoever saves a life, it would be as if he saved the life of all mankind.'

Living donors

Live donation is only possible for 'paired organs' (such as kidneys and lungs) or part of the liver. In recent years there has been a considerable increase in the number of living donors.

The main ethical issue here is that the life and health of the donor should not be unduly jeopardized. As Kant pointed out, we have a primary duty to 'preserve ourselves physically'. So there is potentially something immoral about knowingly endangering one's life or cutting it short since the human body is something 'of importance and worth'. That is why 'free informed consent' is so vital for living donation, and the doctors involved are responsible for not doing anything that might deliberately damage the donor's health. Nowadays the risks involved are generally reckoned to be 'within acceptable levels', though for some donors there may be a long-term possibility of hypertension. However, at least in theory it is important that there should be no element of pressure or coercion on a live donor; and where the donor 'lacks capacity to make an informed decision', we really need some mechanism to help.

Elective ventilation

'Elective ventilation' means starting the incubation and ventilation of a gravely ill patient who is close to death purely in order to facilitate organ donation after brain-stem death. As a procedure it was banned by the Department of Health in 1994 because it was reckoned not to be in the best interests of the patient and therefore unlawful, though this was never tested in the courts. There is a (very small) danger of a patient who would otherwise have died going on 'living' in a profound coma or persistent vegetative state; and because of the general shortage of resources, doing this on a regular basis could mean depriving someone of a ventilator who really needs it. So although in theory elective ventilation might increase the number of organs available, it is not currently regarded as a 'viable option', and any change to the present law would require an effective advanced-decision mechanism.

Therapeutic cloning

This involves the 'use of cell nucleus replacement technology to develop compatible tissue for transplantation' and is rather beyond the scope of this chapter – but will increasingly raise significant ethical issues as research continues and advances are made.

Improving the infrastructure

In 2000 the BMA called for a 'single comprehensive piece of legislation covering all aspects of organ donation'; and in 2008 the Organ Donation Taskforce made 14 recommendations that have led to significant improvements in the 'organizational structure of the organ donation programme'. Its main aim was that 'donation should be a usual (rather than unusual) part of end of life care', and over the five years from 2008 to 2013, donation rates increased by some 50%. Referrals have increased and donation from emergency departments has improved, though relative refusal rates have remained static. Family refusal is the biggest obstacle to donation in the UK.

But evidence from Spain (which has the highest donation rate in the world) and elsewhere suggests that getting the organization of donation right is as important as increasing the overall number of donors. The Spanish system is not directly transferable, but there are still lessons to be learnt about focus, co-ordination and communication. There is potential in this country for many more donations and fewer unnecessary deaths, though the administrative hurdles are formidable. The key to improvement lies somewhere in a combination of improving the 'patient pathway' and increasing public awareness and education.

Of course, the prevention of disease remains an even greater goal, and we need to retain that perspective on organ donation. But as Sue Cansdale points out in a powerful booklet called *Transforming Lives* (compiled after the death of her daughter Zoe and published by the charity Legacy for Life), 'When people realize how much can be done, and discover the comfort of knowing something good came out of their tragedy, there will be no shortage of donors.'

4

Healthcare issues towards the end of life: A chaplain's perspective

Mia Hilborn

I write this chapter as the head of chaplaincy of a large NHS London trust, where I am an independent assessor for the human tissue authority and have served or am serving on various groups, including the clinical ethics advisory group, the organ donation committee, critical care end of life, paediatric end of life, trust end of life, tissue bank, LCP (Liverpool Care Pathway for the dying) and Amber Care Bundle steering group (Assessment, Management, Best practice, Engagement of individuals or carers when Recovery is uncertain).

The chapter will examine some of the issues that point to differences of care and approach to death and dying between an Anglican priest and healthcare professionals. An Anglican priest will have had classical training in virtue, moral, personal and social ethics, been encouraged to reflect on death and dying and will have engaged in practical and pastoral studies. He or she will have experienced years of individual and group

pastoral and religious care within both church and community, and will have a multilayered approach to end
of life care. Clinicians and healthcare professionals are
highly trained in their specialities, generally including
medical law and ethics (the in-depth ethical approach
is an option taken by some clinicians) and will have had
many years of personal experience of patient and relative or carer encounters within the clinical setting and
will continue to spend hours discussing cases within
multidisciplinary teams and peer groups. Some healthcare professionals are extraordinarily skilled in end of life
care: palliative care teams, Macmillan nurses, SNODs
(specialist nurses for organ donation) and others. So
too are some Anglican priests, but most of us find it a
difficult ministerial task.

Healthcare issues I have faced around end of life care
generally have a practical (liturgical, prayerful or pastoral)
response, and also require ethical reflection. Except in
emergency situations, it is usually wiser at the end of life
to listen and pray rather than 'do' and 'sort problems'.
No doubt there are some issues that need addressing,
but calm sacred space is a dignified gift to give to dying
patients and their families or friends, who are in regular contact with various aspects of bustling healthcare
provision. I have been included in conversations about
advanced decision making – where does a person wish
to die, who should be called, funeral planning, organ
donation and so on – in pastorally supporting the dying
and the family, in recognizing cultural issues (which can
include religious issues) such as news-giving, movement

of the body after death and watching as mourners fill in the grave after burial. Issues concerning organ, tissue and body donation are discussed elsewhere, but withdrawal of care, and its timing, are important for final prayers. Emergency weddings can be beautiful and yet achingly sad, as I have had to ensure, with both calmness and action, that the right questions were asked before any paperwork was completed, so that the families would be happy to live with their memories of the weddings. The importance of religious care (pre, at and post death) is highly significant: knowing, for example, how, when and whether to baptize a dying baby, when to offer blessing and how to leave a reminder of the ritual, such as a blessing card for the dying. Similarly, care of families where there is a mix of religions or beliefs can be challenging: how to offer appropriate rites while retaining one's religious integrity. Opportunities for religious and spiritual care are manifold: truth-telling and reinforcing news, contract funerals; bereavement support of the family, carers or staff; supporting, maybe for many years, those who witness a particularly traumatic or emotionally complicated death; memorial services and providing opportunities for the community to grieve, honour and remember their dead; supporting healthcare staff who work regularly with the dying and their families or who have experienced death within their domestic or social lives; learning and remembering lessons about emotional and spiritual support and preparing for the future, which includes end of life for all. Clinicians also encounter these issues but their focus is the treatment and care of their patients and their ethical approach is frequently different from the Church's approach.

Clinical ethics

Clinical ethics are taught to clinicians to help them with the difficult decisions they must make in healthcare. The basic medical ethical principles are to do no harm and to offer beneficial treatment (beneficence). The ethical methodology used is different from that experienced by those classically trained in theological colleges: it is practical, applied speedily and is much less detailed. A common teaching method is to make use of case studies, encouraging students to apply principles in a systematic manner. One of the main ways this happens in the UK and the USA is by the use of answers to questions, often using: 'clinical integrity', 'beneficence', 'autonomy' and 'justice/non-maleficence' (Beauchamp and Childress, 2009); or the 'four quadrant' approach, namely 'medical indications', 'patient preferences', 'quality of life' and 'contextual features' (Ethics Consultation in Portland, 2006). Other ethical indicators may also be used, such as 'sanctity of life', 'acts/omissions distinction', 'doctrine of double effect', 'contextualization' (UK Clinical Ethics Network, 2013).

Healthcare professionals of all kinds are often introduced to end of life ethics by the use of 'the trolley on the train track' illustration, first introduced by the British philosopher Philippa Foot (Thomson, 1985, p. 1395).

The idea is that an individual is driving a trolley and suddenly sees five men on the track directly in front. The trolley can't stop in time and the five people are unable to get off the track. The trolley could divert to another track but it would mean killing one person on the alternative track who also can't move and would definitely be crushed. Students are asked if it is morally permissible to kill the one to save the five, and the vast majority of people the world over say it is. A slightly different form of the question is often then introduced. There is a bridge over the track and a hugely obese person is standing on the bridge. If the person fell on to the track the huge body would stop the trolley and save either the five people or the one person. Should you then murder the obese person by pushing them on to the track or try to talk the person into jumping to save the others? What if there were five children on the track, and the hugely obese person was 'palliative' (nearing the end of life)? There are obvious implications to be drawn from this imaginative tale for healthcare: the limited amount of money that can be spent on sick patients and the ethical decisions that have to be made day to day as to who receives care. I have been present at discussions where it has been suggested that hugely obese persons obviously don't care much about their lives or they wouldn't be hugely obese, so it wouldn't matter much to them; that you save the 'least sick' first in a dire emergency but the most sick normally (this is the general method used in emergency departments: the sicker you are the quicker you are treated), but in a mass incident or in a pandemic situation it is recognized that ethics may have to change to meet mass health-care needs. The majority of healthcare professionals theoretically would not wish either to murder a person or to force one person to give his or her life to save others, and would strive to find other solutions.

In contrast to this ad hoc approach to emergency life-and-death situations, the ethical concepts used day to day by healthcare professionals in end of life care that were noted at the beginning of this section are described below.

Clinical integrity

This is particularly relevant where a clinician has concerns between what the patient and family want and what is clinically 'reasonable'. For example, a patient may have had a massive heart attack leading to brain damage but the family might insist that he or she will experience a miracle and so they will refuse withdrawal of care. There may be differences between the care offered in different hospitals or there could be issues about disclosing infor-mation (e.g. HIV status when a family clearly does not know a patient is dying of an AIDS-related condition). How does the doctor retain their integrity in an ethically 'messy' situation?

Beneficence

Beneficence is concerned with what actually brings benefit to the patient, or what would help the family. For example, a patient may be clinically dead but a family member could be travelling from another country, so it is decided to keep the patient on life support until all family members have said their goodbyes; this is then withdrawn, perhaps after appropriate religious support. Sometimes disputes with families occur when additional treatment is deemed clinically futile. Families can get severely distressed when watching resuscitation, and beg doctors to continue even though it is medically futile to do so. The possibility of such reactions from families means that normally they are removed from resuscitation areas during active treatment. Sometimes I have been asked to support families waiting for news during such times of extreme anxiety.

Autonomy

There can often be concerns about what is in the best interests of the patient. Is the patient being coerced or do they have limited capacity? If so, are they able to make appropriate independent decisions? Both clinicians and chaplains need to be aware of the Mental Capacity Act (Office of the Public Guardian, 2005). The main principles of the Act state that all adults have the right to make decisions for themselves unless unable to do so, and should be supported as much as possible to make those decisions, even if this is deemed unwise or strange. If a person lacks capacity, any decisions or actions should be in their best interests, while people who lack capacity should not be restricted unnecessarily. Medical staff can act against the wishes of a person (for example, re-suscitation of a patient in A&E even if the patient has shouted they don't want it) if they have a 'reasonable belief that the person lacks capacity' (p. 14). For emergency weddings, no one but the patient is allowed to give consent, and there must be no dispute about their capacity to give that consent.

Justice/non-maleficence

Concern might be raised about a patient's safety, about the protection of others (such as minors) and potential conflicts of interest. There may be justice issues or stewardship implications about the use of very expensive treatment when commissioners have to decide on budget implications (Beauchamp and Childress, 2009).

The four quadrant approach: medical indication

If employed, this approach should be followed step by step, generally in order. First, all the medical and clinical indicators are examined. What are the reasonable diagnostic and treatment options available? For each of the different treatment options available, what is the prognosis? The UK Clinical Ethics Network uses the four quadrant approach to give an example case for clinical ethics committees (UK Clinical Ethics Network, 2013). As each treatment option is considered, are the goals of the medicine fulfilled? How likely is it that the goals will be achieved or could the treatment be futile? Such considerations are often discussed when a palliative patient may or may not be offered further sessions of chemotherapy. If the goal of treatment is no longer curative, is the treatment appropriate for a dying patient?

Patient preferences

A first concern is whether or not a patient has sufficient capacity to express preferences. If competent, what does the patient prefer? If not competent, which option would be in their best interests bearing in mind their values and opinions (if known)? What do relatives/carers say? I have sometimes had a role in ensuring that the wishes of the unconscious patient were made known and, when necessary, have spoken on behalf of or have supported distressed relatives expressing their views. It may take considerable time to discover who is able to decide on a patient's behalf, and so I can listen and try to help families come to a reasonable compromise when there are cultural or religious divisions within the family that have led to multiple opinions about, for example, withdrawal of care or donation of organs.

If the patient is conscious it is important that the process used to ascertain their wishes about treatment plans or end of life options leads to informed consent. That normally means that a doctor has taken the time to explain fully the reasons for the treatment, how it will happen and the possible risks. The doctor should ensure that the patient has understood what is said to them, and that they have agreed voluntarily and without duress or coercion, or without any material or financial pressure. A person may be perceived to be coerced into refusing life-sustaining treatment due to family pressure. This could be related to housing (next of kin wanting the person's home to live in or to sell), it could be that the family does not want to look after a sick person or there could be monetary issues, for example paying for a university place for a student in return for giving a kidney as a living donor, which is illegal in the UK. Part of the role of the priest is to care for the sick and the dying, to ensure dignity of care, respect and love, and it is appropriate to check carefully where end of life decisions are concerned. An effective way of doing this is to ask the patient what the doctor has said and what has been decided, and then reflect that back in pastoral conversation and prayer. If there is some discord or gaps in memory, it implies the patient may not have understood or could be unhappy with the decision, and further conversations may be required.

Quality of life

A pivotal question is: Would the patient's quality of life be increased by the treatment option or at least remain the same? If not, why is the treatment being considered? It is noticeable, anecdotally at least, that doctors who have cancer will opt to forgo 'extra' treatments especially at the end of life, when such often painful treatments may increase life by days or weeks; whereas I have sadly sometimes witnessed the relatives of non-medical people begging for every possible treatment option, even when they can cause an increase of physical discomfort to the patient. The concept of futility seems to vary according to experience of number of deaths seen: someone who has seen more deaths, such as a healthcare professional, can decide earlier in the end of life care to stop treatment than families of those desperate to keep their loved one alive, for whom the whole process of watching them die is terrifying. In such circumstances I have tried to work with the family, supporting and helping them choose what to accept and what to fight, while keeping the well-being of the patient always in the forefront. There are cultures where fighting for every possible treatment, often accompanied by loud and frequent bouts of intense crying, are seen as signs of love. African Christian women have explained to me that, when community members are present, if they do not fight so aggressively for their dying husband's continued treatment, and display excessive emotion before and after death, culturally it will be said that they did not love their husbands. White western families have also been seen to push for every treatment option available, against medical advice about futility, in families where there has been no discernible spiritual support nor common understanding of the significance of death among family members. There can also be unresolved emotional relationship issues, which may mean that the trauma of impending death is being dealt with by a fragmented and emotionally and spiritually unstable family. Those dying people who have clear, kind, religious and spiritual support at pre-palliative and during the end of life phase often have fewer hospital admissions and are more likely to have a peaceful death. People who are enabled to have control over their spiritual lives and have the support of their community tend to have improved well-being, even at the end of life (Krause, 2013). At such distressing times I have tried to listen to relatives, talk through with them what the doctors have said to help them realize some of the implications of what they are asking for, since relatives can sometimes be in greater shock than the dying person. Similarly, I may speak to the doctors on the patient's or relatives' behalf and try to explain both sides and then 'hold' the family spiritually while externalizing some of the turmoil through religious rites and spoken prayer. Quite literally pouring holy oil on a troubled brow, asking for peace at the end of life, out loud, can figuratively remind all concerned about the soul's need for peace, forgiveness and end of strife. Sometimes it is the clinicians who have not realized that the family feel the time for active treatment has come to an end and wish for the patient to die peacefully, as pain-free as possible and with dignity. Then I respectfully draw the doctors' attention to the concept of futility at such times.

Healthcare issues towards the end of life

Contextual features

These features should recognize the impact of religious, emotional, financial, legal, scientific and educational factors. Whether these should be taken into account at all will depend on the individual circumstances of the patient. I might have a religious role in explaining certain aspects of religious significance – for example, I might call in a Jewish chaplain to give advice about withdrawal of care. As an Anglican, my role could be to support the family through their discussions and decision making, in addition to giving any religious rites, and to explain to the multidisciplinary team (MDT) the reasons behind apparently unusual family responses to planned treatment or withdrawal of care. It is not uncommon that requests for emergency weddings or civil partnerships come when end of life finally appears inevitable, particularly when the partner has no housing rights or where there is no will. Some delicate negotiations may have to take place about appropriate medication to enable the patient to be conscious and give consent rather than risk coercion through vulnerability. Sometimes it can appear that the family's and the dying person's needs clash, and sensitivity and discernment need to be used while at the same time moving at speed to get appropriate paperwork completed. Contextual features can appear, at first sight, lightweight, yet may be pivotal arbitrators in having a good death and keeping the family memory enduringly good and ensuring their social and spiritual protection and security for the rest of their lives.

Sanctity of life

From a clinical perspective this is not necessarily a key principle; rather it could be considered a religious one. It may reasonably be assumed that a religious person would view all human life as having worth and therefore believe it would be wrong to take life in any circumstances. This divergence in understanding the sacredness of human life is at the heart of the difference between Christian and secular understanding of health. The Christian has an incarnational theology: the saviour Jesus Christ himself died and did not save himself, even though he had the ability to do so. He did heal others, including raising some dead people to life, but there is no single Christian healing 'blanket response' to a person who is seriously ill or facing death, despite the claims of 'health, wealth and prosperity gospel' proclaimers. The pure medical perspective does not have to recognize the complexities of faith or belief-based theologies, and may assume religious attitudes to be similar to minor cultural customs – they should be documented if relevant to the individual patient but there is no real need to take account of them in a wider context as this might unnecessarily complicate decision making or simply be irrelevant. Medical time with a patient is short and there is much to be examined, discussed and explained; spiritual issues are simply one of many competing issues. For a further discussion of these issues, see Chapter 1.

Acts/omissions distinction

This is a possibly contentious area in medical ethics where end of life is concerned. The acts or omissions distinction is the difference between, for example, actively killing someone (as in assisted suicide) and not giving life-giving care (such as a 'DNACPR' [Do Not Attempt Cardiopulmonary Resuscitation] order, when a person is not treated after having a heart attack). 'Withholding treatment would only be permissible if a patient's quality of life was so poor and the burden of treatment so great, that it would not be in the patient's best interest to continue treatment' (UK Clinical Ethics Network, 2013). There are fine distinctions to be made between what is or is not withholding of treatment, or indeed what constitutes treatment (such as food and hydration), as has been seen in the debate over the Liverpool Care Pathway review (Department of Health, 2013). Families can be extremely distressed when food and hydration are lawfully withheld from a dying patient. In such circumstances a chaplain can act as both a listening ear and a voice when distress is apparent. In the UK the medical team has the legal responsibility to offer or withdraw care; normal practice is to take into account patient and relative/carer views, if known. This might be thought of as implying that there may be different types of care offered to those who are articulate, with active carers or relatives, compared with those who have no one and do not speak for themselves, but there is no substantial evidence for this. Nonetheless, there is evidence that isolation leads to poorer health outcomes (Cornwell and Waite, 2009).

Doctrine of double effect

In the context of end of life care this is the 'moral distinction between acting with intention to bring about a person's death and performing an act where death is a foreseen but unintended consequence' (UK Clinical Ethics Network, 2013). As already noted, there can be a difference between what is ethically acceptable and what is legally permissible (Silverman, 2011), and it is widely accepted in medicine that intention is more important ethically than outcome. For example, for a patient nearing the end of life with uncontrollable pain, is it permissible to give a pain-killing injection of analgesia that will have the foreseen but unintentional consequence of hastening the death of an unconscious patient? From the Anglican and most medical perspectives this would be ethically acceptable, but from within Hinduism and some eastern faith traditions it may not be welcomed, as people may wish to be conscious before death in order to concentrate on their beliefs in and prayers for reincarnation.

When to give spiritual or religious care

The timing for a Christian patient to receive spiritual care can be difficult while receiving active medical care, yet spiritual care might be time-critical: confession, anointing and communion can only be given to a conscious patient, similarly for the sacrament of the sick for a Roman Catholic. Final prayers or a blessing can be said when the patient is unconscious, and prayers and appropriate blessing can be said after death. Observant and African or Asian Anglicans from all theological spectrums within the denomination will often request anointing and holy communion when they are close to death. Non-observant patients (who don't attend church but say they are Church of England) are likely to ask for prayer, or their relatives ask for final prayers after the patient becomes unconscious. Indeed, I have spent many hours waiting for a patient to slip into unconsciousness as their relatives have articulated that final prayers may only be said when the patient is no longer conscious, so that he or she shouldn't be worried. The deathbed is not the place for a confrontation about spiritual care with grieving relatives, but the role of the relatives as gate-keepers of the dying can be a challenge to appropriate and timely spiritual care. Whenever I have preached about organ donation, for example, individuals have spoken to me afterwards describing having been at a dying relative's bedside, and the patient had wanted to donate, but they had stopped them and were now regretting that.

At the end of the day

With sudden or unexpected death, relatives have their own emotional and spiritual trauma to deal and live with; the shock to them is enormous and it is almost impossible to act 'normally' or 'rationally'. In some ways the Muslim tradition that sees a senior male member of the extended family making emergency deathbed decisions, enabling the immediate relatives to look after the patient without having to 'think' at such a shocking time, is perhaps a kind alternative. However, this person will not have had any medical or clinical preparation before becoming involved, and therefore might not be fully aware of circumstances leading to withdrawal of care, thus adding another layer of emotional and spiritual difficulty for all concerned. The western legal notion of next of kin can also clash with family-orientated decision making.

Figure 1 helpfully illustrates the different trajectories of dying for four major palliative profiles for older adults. Each will need different types of care at the different stages. There will be some crossover; for example, all will need a funeral, but the types of prayers and readings chosen may reflect the manner of both life and death, the prayers used for a suicide or sudden death perhaps being very different from those used when a person has struggled with chronic illness or increased frailty for several years.

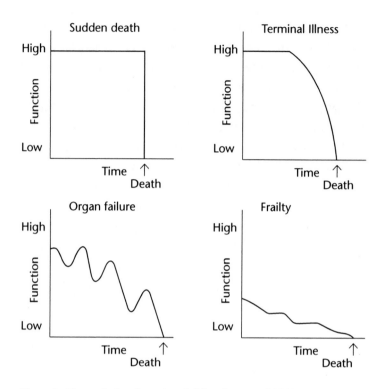

Figure 1: Theoretical trajectories of dying (Lunney, 2002)

The role of the priest

The role of the priest or the chaplain can be to act as a spiritual friend to the bereaved patient and the bereaved, through the stages of death and the grief cycle. The person is likely to have periods of spiritual distress, despair, longing; they may wish to review their life goals and look again at individual meaning based upon spiritual and emotional changes, either as they come nearer to their time of death, or for relatives and friends during their period of mourning and bereavement. Part of the priest's role is to represent the communal memory of the person who has died, in the funeral and then during memorial services, in the liturgical year on days such as All Souls, and by being the custodian of names in a church memorial book. A decision would need to be made for each dying person about which stages are needed and how the approach and facilitation of the discussion should be made, what type of religious care should be offered, how the family and the religious community should be supported, and how to recognize that a memory held by the religious community and the domestic family or friends is being created. At or near death the dying person needs honesty and clarity, questions need answering or discussions need to be held, and the end of the journey needs to be reflected on in thought-filled new and ancient prayer, Scripture and ritual. I have found it helpful to look back upon my own pastoral and religious care of the dying and reflect, testing whether my redemptive theology, ecclesiology and incarnational theology have all come together. Have my own ethical standards and integrity been upheld while caring for a person at the end of life? Can I honestly live with myself when I have been as honest as I can be after being with a dying human being? It is good practice to use reflective practice or Ignatian reflection after caring for a dying person, to try to learn how to do better in the future.

In conclusion, the Anglican priest and the healthcare professional have markedly different ethical underpinnings and roles at end of life, but both have the dying person's best interests at heart. I feel my role is multilayered, and ethical principles are needed to ensure that the dying person is helped in the best way possible. Death is distressing but I feel my role, in part, can help to make sure it is the best it can be; where, on reflection, both the dying person and family are glad of the Anglican rites, rituals and care that bring peace and comfort and hope in the midst of the sadness of death.

References

Amber Care Bundle, www.ambercarebundle.org/homepage.aspx.

Anderson, Megory, *Sacred Dying: Creating Rituals for Embracing the End of Life,* New York, Marlowe & Company, 2003.

Anderson, Megory, *Attending the Dying: A Handbook of Practical Guidelines,* Harrisburg, PA, Morehouse Publishing, 2005.

Beauchamp, Tom L. and Childress, James Franklin, *Principles of Biomedical Ethics,* Oxford, Oxford University Press, 2009.

Cornwell, Erin Y. and Waite, Linda J., 'Social Disconnectedness, Perceived Isolation, and Health among Older Adults', *Journal of Health and Social Behaviour,* 2009, 50.1, pp. 31–48.

Department of Health, 'More Care, Less Pathway: A Review of the Liverpool Care Pathway', 15 July 2013.

Department of Health, 'Snapshot Review of Complaints in End of Life Care', 15 July 2013.

Edmonds, David, 'Matters of Life and Death', *Prospect,* 7 October 2010, www.prospectmagazine.co.uk/magazine/ethics-trolley-problem/#.Ui4ulElwbIU.

www.endoflifecare.nhs.uk/care-pathway/step-1-discussions-as-the-end-of-life-approaches/amber-care-bundle.aspx.

Ethics Consultation in Portland, Catholic Health Association of the United States, *Health Progress,* March–April 2006, pp. 36–41,

https://sftest.chausa.org/docs/default-source/health-progress/
ethics-consultation-in-portland-pdf.pdf.pdf?sfvrsn=0.

General Medical Council, www.gmc-uk.org/Treatment_and_care_
towards_the_end_of_life___English_0513.pdf_48902105.pdf.

Krause, N. and Hayward, R. D., 'Church-based Social Support,
Functional Disability, and Change in Personal Control Over Time',
Journal of Religion and Health, 2014, 53.1, pp. 267–78 (published
online April 2013).

Lunney, J. R., 2002, at http://origin-ars.els-cdn.com/content/
image/1-s2.0-S152284010700033X-gr2.jpg.

Lunney, J. R., Lynn, J. and Hogan, C., 'Profiles of Older Medicare
Decedents', *Journal of the American Geriatrics Society*, 2002, 50,
pp. 1108–12.

Lunney, J. R. et al., 'Patterns of Functional Decline at the End of
Life', *Journal of the American Medical Association*, 2003, 289.18,
pp. 2387–92.

Office of the Public Guardian, *The Mental Capacity Act: Making
Decisions ... About Your Health, Welfare or Finances. Who decides
when you can't?* 2005.

Roberts, Stephen B., *Professional, Spiritual and Pastoral Care*, Wood-
stock, VT, Skylight Paths Publishing, 2012.

Silverman, Henry, 'Protecting Vulnerable Subjects in Critical Care
Trials: Enhancing the Informed Consent Process and Recommendations for Safeguards', *Annals of Intensive Care*, 2011, 1.8,
pp. 1–7.

Thomson, Judith J., 'The Trolley Problem', *The Yale Law Journal*, 1985,
94.6, pp. 1395–415.

UK Clinical Ethics Network, 2013, www.ukcen.net/uploads/docs/
ethical_issues/endlife.pdf.

A selection of key Church of England documents on end of life issues

Response to the Director of Public Prosecutions' Policy for Prosecutors in Respect of Cases of Encouraging or Assisting Suicide, 25 February 2010

The Mission and Public Affairs Division of the Church of England has responded to the Director of Public Prosecutions' Policy for Prosecutors in Respect of Cases of Encouraging or Assisting Suicide:

The Church of England acknowledges the difficult task given to the DPP by the Law Lords and we wish to express our appreciation for the manner in which he has undertaken his task which has included a period of comprehensive public consultation.

We continue to oppose any change in the law with regard to assisted suicide and we are assured by the DPP that the guidelines do not represent any such change. Assisted suicide remains a crime and, as with all crimes, there remains a presumption in favour of prosecution.

At the end of the day

These guidelines do not provide blanket immunity from prosecution, nor do they give prior permission to break the law. It is right that there is no clear line drawn which will allow anybody assisting a suicide to know in advance whether they will be prosecuted. These guidelines are intended to weigh a complex set of different factors which, of their nature, can only be assessed after the fact not before it.

Assisted suicide, as well as being a crime, is always also a tragedy. We empathize with those who struggle with their own illness and suffering as well as with those who struggle with the illnesses and suffering of those they love most. We believe, however, that the most compassionate course is to provide love, support and the best possible medical and nursing care, not to acquiesce in requests for assisted suicide. Compassion does not always mean saying 'yes'. Protecting the vulnerable, ensuring that every life is appreciated as being valuable and maintaining the indispensable bond of trust between health professionals and patients outweighs arguments in favour of individual choice. In a truly caring and moral society, increased autonomy for the few ought never to be pursued at the cost of placing an increased burden on the many.

We also recognize that, in certain, restricted circumstances, prosecution may not be the most appropriate way of responding to assisted suicide. The DPP's guidelines reflect this even though we do not agree with all of them as we made clear in our submission during the consultation process.

We commend, however, the changes made from the interim guidelines in removing the presence of terminal illness, disability and degenerative physical conditions as factors to be taken into consideration when coming to a decision whether or not to prosecute. We also welcome the removal of a victim's history of attempted suicide as a factor against prosecution. The pressures that spouses and sole carers have to live with, and the influence that this may bring to bear on their decision-making, have also been reflected in changes made from the interim guidelines. We view as a positive step the inclusion of health professionals who assist suicide in the list of factors favouring prosecution. Abandoning the methodology of 'weighting' factors to be taken into consideration is sensible and enables a focused 'case by case' approach to be taken.

The DPP has highlighted compassion in his guidelines and he has introduced clarity in the application of the law prohibiting assisted suicide. We believe that this ought to bring to an end calls for a change in the law. Any further calls for change would be ideologically driven and, if heeded, would change fundamentally and irrevocably the moral status of our society and would make this a less compassionate and caring land in which to live and die.

Response to the Report of the Commission on Assisted Dying, January 2012

After some months' delay, the Commission on Assisted Dying has issued its report. Its recommendations fall short of seeking wide-ranging changes in the law on assisted suicide, advocating instead a form of physician-assisted suicide for terminally ill individuals who are judged to be competent to make such requests in a voluntary and informed manner. While this may disappoint those who wish to see assisted suicide made more widely available, it still represents an unacceptable threat to the wellbeing of hundreds of thousands of vulnerable people.

The commission is a self-appointed group, chosen by Lord Falconer, a noted advocate of a change in the law on assisted suicide. No one who had a principled objection to assisted suicide was invited to act as a commissioner, yet eight of the original eleven other commissioners appointed by Lord Falconer were known to favour some form of assisted suicide. Such a commission, funded by individuals who also wish to legitimize assisted suicide, cannot be considered to be 'independent'. It is, therefore, unsurprising that the commission has claimed that it has found a basis for changing the law to allow a form of assisted suicide without placing vulnerable individuals at increased risk.

The core issue with regard to risk, however, has not been satisfactorily addressed by the commission: are vulnerable individuals at greater risk of abuse under

Lord Falconer's proposals or under the current law? The reason for this omission is straightforward: any change in the law to permit assisted suicide is bound to put vulnerable people at increased risk. In effect, what Lord Falconer has done is to argue that it is morally acceptable to put many vulnerable people at increased risk so that the aspirations of a small number of individuals, to control the time, place and means of their deaths, might be met. Such a calculus of risk is wholly unacceptable.

The commission's thinking is, at times, both contentious and contradictory. For example, it states that *'the current legal status of assisted suicide is inadequate, incoherent and should not continue'*, but it also recommends that for all cases of assisted suicide that fall outside its proposed guidelines, the status quo ought to continue to be implemented. It also states, incorrectly that *'the current policy on assisted suicide accepts the principle of compassionate assistance with suicide'*. It does not; it accepts that compassion may be viewed as a mitigating factor in cases of assisted suicide, set alongside other mitigating as well as exacerbating factors. It complains that assisted suicide is an *'amateur activity'* as if that, in itself, is an argument for turning it into a professional activity. Somewhat tautologically, it states, *'People criminalized by the legal prohibition on assisted suicide are currently treated as criminal suspects'*, while accepting that an amended law criminalizing assisted suicide ought to remain in place.

The commission wishes to limit assisted suicide to terminally ill people, with terminal illness understood as, '*an advanced, progressive, incurable condition that is likely to lead to the patient's death within the next twelve months.*' This is to make a statistical lottery of the lives of individuals. While doctors are able to state with accuracy the *average* life expectancy of individuals with any given illness, they are not able to state the actual life expectancy of any given individual. How '*likely*' must a prognosis be to allow a life to be ended?

In its principles for framing safeguards against abuse, the commission argues that '*the assessment, advice, support and independent judgements of two independent doctors*' ought to be central to any decision-making process. This, in spite of the fact that the medical profession is opposed to any participation in assisted suicide. Doctors are not only to assess and support individuals whom they deem competent to request assisted suicide, they are also to write lethal prescriptions to enable their lives to end. With the majority of doctors opposed to playing any part in this procedure, how might 'independent' doctors be found to engage in the process? The answer is likely to be that a relatively small number of doctors, in favour of assisted suicide, would feature disproportionately in such cases, bringing into question their objectivity and 'independence'.

A further proposed safeguard is that '*the person has a settled intention to die*'. In order to ensure that this is the case the commission has recommended a 'cooling-off' period of two weeks, that may in some circumstances be reduced to six days. While accepting that a request for assisted suicide ought to come after a process of consultation, a two week 'cooling off period' is woe-fully inadequate. It would be a strange reflection of our society if ending a life were treated in the same way as applying for a car loan.

The greatest concerns, however, centre on what the commission has termed, 'voluntariness and absence of coercion'. It is worrying that in this regard the com-mission is opposed to a person contemplating assisted suicide being *'unduly influenced by others'*. What, it might reasonably be asked, constitutes undue influence?

Nonetheless, the commission does state, *'The Com-mission accepts that there is a real risk that some individuals might come under pressure to request an assisted death if this option should become available, including direct pressures from family members or medical professionals, indirect pressures caused by societal discrimination or lack of availability of resources for care and support, and self-imposed pressures that could result from the individuals having low self-worth or feeling themselves to be a burden on others. The Commission does not accept that any of these forms of pressure could be a legitimate motivation for a ter-minally ill individual to seek an assisted death. Therefore, it is essential that any future system should contain safe-guards designed to ensure, as much as possible, that any decision to seek an assisted suicide is a genuinely voluntary and autonomous choice, not influenced by another per-son's wishes, or by constrained social circumstances, such as lack of access to adequate end of life care and support.'*

The commission states that adequate safeguards ought to be put in place to ensure that consent is full and informed and without coercion, but singularly fails to provide them. It is known, for example, that it may take as long as six months to rule out a diagnosis of clinical depression; a condition that the commission accepts is a barrier to accepting a request for assisted suicide. Is it seriously to be expected that an individual who believes that he or she has only a few months to live will be properly assessed for depression over a six month period by 'independent' doctors who are unlikely to be psychiatrists? In the UK some six hundred thousand people are believed to suffer from dependent personality disorder, a known risk factor in suicide. A proper assessment and diagnosis of this condition is not easily achieved, especially without the expert input of psychologists, who rightly insist that diagnostic tests are separated by some months in order to obtain an accurate diagnosis. People with this disorder, especially if other factors add to their vulnerability, may easily be prey to being *'unduly influenced by others'*, without their condition being apparent to the doctors who assess them.

It is the elderly, however, who will be placed at greatest risk, especially those nearing the end of their lives. Over a third of a million elderly people suffer 'elder abuse' each year, with a further hundred thousand suffering neglect. More than half of the perpetrators of this abuse are close relatives and in one quarter of cases financial gain is the major motive. These are large figures, representing huge areas of need and vulnerability. (While exact figures are hard to determine because of the possibility of unreported cases, on average about thirty people from the UK die each year as a result of assisted suicide.) It is naïve to the point of neglect to believe that people who already abuse elderly people, especially for financial gain, will not seek to exploit any change in the law permitting assisted suicide. Elderly people, suffering abuse, will with justification, fear any sign of illness as another pretext for mistreatment.

The commission recommends that all cases of physician-assisted suicide ought to be carefully monitored and that a statutory body ought to review every individual case for compliance with the law. This suggests that 'mistakes' will occur; it will, of course, be too late for a review body to undo the harm done.

It is also naïve to believe that monitoring procedures will be properly adhered to. After decades of practising assisted suicide and euthanasia, the report rate is only 80% in the Netherlands and in Belgium it is just above 50%. To put this in context, NHS hospitals require staff to adhere to hand-washing procedures in at least 95% of all circumstances. To expect a higher threshold for hand-washing than for ending a person's life is manifestly absurd. There is simply no way of knowing how many people have died in the Netherlands or in Belgium outside of their 'safeguards'. It would be naïve in the extreme to believe that the situation would be any different in the UK.

The systemic and endemic neglect and abuse of vulnerable people in some Care Homes, highlighted in a government report in December 2010, have, quite rightly, been seen as national scandals. This neglect and abuse occurred in a heavily regulated and supposedly well-monitored service. It beggars belief to suggest that the sort of people who abuse and neglect vulnerable adults in Care Homes, or those who fail to monitor the service properly, would be particular in monitoring and reporting adherence to safeguards that might be put in place to protect vulnerable individuals from the effects of legitimising assisted suicide.

The Commission on Assisted Dying set itself a bold objective: to find a safe way of amending the law to permit some forms of assisted suicide. In spite of its labours, it has manifestly failed to so.

Revd Dr Brendan McCarthy

Church of England – Mission and Public Affairs Council Response to 'Safeguarding Choice: A Draft Assisted Dying Bill for Consultation', November 2012

The Mission and Public Affairs Council of the Church of England is the body responsible for overseeing research and comment on social and political issues on behalf of the Church. The Council comprises a representative group of bishops, clergy and lay people with interest and expertise in the relevant areas, and reports to the General Synod through the Archbishops' Council.

The Mission and Public Affairs Council presents a Christian ethos, drawing on the witness of the Christian Scriptures and reflecting on Christian tradition and contemporary thought. Belief in God as Creator and Redeemer, in human beings' intrinsic value as creatures made in the Image of God and in the imperatives of love and justice, underpins the Council's approach. The Council believes that the ethical and social principles developed from this foundation have a value and relevance in society that can be acknowledged by those of other faiths or none.

1.1 We welcome the opportunity to respond to this consultation. We note that, in the consultation document, Question One addresses the issue of the desirability of changing the current law on assisted suicide while the remaining questions address means by which individuals might be safeguarded against abuse were the law to be changed in the manner proposed by the Choice at the End of Life All Party Parliamentary Group.

1.2 The Church of England's policy with regard to assisted suicide has been most recently stated in a motion passed at General Synod in February 2012. This motion included the clause, that Synod:

'affirm the intrinsic value of every human life and express its support for the current law on assisted suicide as a means of contributing to a just and compassionate society in which vulnerable people are protected'.

1.3 Consequently, we believe that it is appropriate, in this response, to answer Question One in the consultation document (*If adequate safeguards can be found to allow assisted dying (assistance to die for terminally ill, mentally competent adults only) and no healthcare* *professional is obliged in any way to assist a patient to die, would you support a change in the law on assisted dying?*), but decline to answer questions that seek to contribute to changing the current law on assisted suicide.

2.1 While acknowledging that the draft bill seeks genuinely to meet the stated wishes of a small number of people, we believe that it fails sufficiently to recognise its potentially damaging consequences.

2.2 It is essential that society values and affirms the life and wellbeing of each of its members, regardless of age, illness, disability or economic or social status. A change in the law on assisted suicide has the capacity to undermine this by suggesting that society may be complicit in some individuals deliberately and actively ending others' lives prematurely. Important health and social care messages and interventions such as those aimed at suicide prevention or at giving reassurance of compassionate and effective End of Life Care are difficult to reconcile with a law that would enable health professionals to participate in actively ending patients' lives. A law permitting assisted suicide would run counter to the purpose and tenor of positive initiatives aimed at affirming and valuing vulnerable individuals and groups including numerous elderly people, many individuals living with disability, those who are socially isolated or who suffer from low self-esteem as well as individuals and families coping with issues related to dementia.

2.3 A change in the law would negatively redefine the concept of health care in England and Wales and would significantly and detrimentally alter the nature of the relationship between health professionals and patients, a point pertinently made by a number of professional bodies.

2.4 Crucially, a change in the law would permit people actively to participate in bringing about the deaths of other individuals, something that, apart from cases of self-defence, has not formed part of the legal landscape of the United Kingdom since the abolition of capital punishment. The draft bill seeks specifically to create, in law, a new practice of 'assisted dying' in which an individual who is given assistance in ending his or her life is deemed not to have committed suicide. This would be a legal fiction: ending one's life is, by definition, suicide and it would be both disingenuous and confusing to suggest otherwise.

2.5 Such consequences would have far-reaching and damaging effects on the nature of our society; a price too great to pay for whatever perceived benefits they might arguably bring to a few.

3.1 While recognizing that individuals who wish to have assistance in ending their own lives may be seen as being vulnerable, their position needs to be considered alongside the obvious vulnerability of more than 300,000 elderly people who suffer abuse each year in England and Wales, very many of them at the hands of their own family members, often for pecuniary reasons. The question must be asked: on balance, might a change in the law place more vulnerable people at increased risk of neglect, marginalization or abuse? Unless the answer can be a demonstrable and convincing 'no' it would be

negligent in the extreme to contemplate such a change.
3.2 Recent revelations with regard to neglect and abuse of elderly people in some care homes and current disquiet at whether the Liverpool Care Pathway and 'Do not attempt resuscitation' protocols are consistently applied in a correct manner indicate that even carefully constructed and reputedly well-monitored practices can be prone to lapses and perhaps even deliberate circumvention. There is nothing to cause us to believe that a law permitting assisted suicide would not encounter similar problems.

4.1 Medical professionals have consistently pointed out that it is extremely difficult to place an accurate timescale on terminal illness, especially at the point of initial diagnosis (the moment identified in the Draft Bill as marking the start of a twelve month period during which it is 'reasonably expected' that a patient will die). 'Reasonable expectation' is an excessively subjective criterion to apply to matters of life and death, and leaves the path open for error and, even, deliberate complicity.

5.1 In addition to difficulties associated with direct and (more probably) indirect pressure being placed on vulnerable people to consider assisted suicide, there is an inherent flaw in the concept of individuals having a 'settled mind' to end their lives.

People with the strongest and most 'settled' convictions have been known to change their minds if given time and opportunity to do so. Many individuals who have attempted to end their lives, but who were revived or rescued, sometimes against their expressed wishes, have subsequently gone on to live happy and constructive lives, glad that their 'settled' opinion did not result in their intended goal of premature death. Assisted suicide allows no such recourse to a second chance. This is particularly worrying where the entire 'decision-making' process is to be compressed within a proposed twelve month time-frame.

6.1 In addition to the concerns outlined above, we have concerns about the particular safeguards proposed in the Draft Bill. So, for all these reasons, we continue to support the current law on assisted suicide and the nuanced and compassionate way in which it is administered.

Philip Fletcher
Chairman, Mission and Public Affairs Council

Response of the Mission and Public Affairs Council of the Church of England to The National Health Service Blood and Transplant Consultation on Organ Donation Post 2013 Strategy, 20 September 2012

The Mission and Public Affairs Council of the Church of England is the body responsible for overseeing research and comment on social and political issues on behalf of the Church. The Council comprises a representative group of bishops, clergy and lay people with interest and expertise in the relevant areas, and reports to the General Synod through the Archbishops' Council.

At the end of the day

> *The Mission and Public Affairs Council presents a Christian ethos, drawing on the witness of the Christian Scriptures and reflecting on Christian tradition and contemporary thought. Belief in God as Creator and Redeemer, in human beings' intrinsic value as creatures made in the Image of God and in the imperatives of love and justice, underpins the Council's approach. The Council believes that the ethical and social principles that are developed from this foundation may be embraced by people of other faiths or of none.*

Background

1.1 The Church of England affirms that *'giving one's self and one's possessions voluntarily for the wellbeing of others and without compulsion is a Christian duty of which organ donation is a striking example. Christians have a mandate to heal, motivated by compassion, mercy, knowledge and ability. The Christian tradition both affirms the God-given value of human bodily life, and the principle of putting the needs of others before one's own needs.'*[1] This forms the context for our response to the current NHSBT consultation.

1.2 A number of important messages emerge from the NHSBT consultation background paper, *'Organ Donation*

---

1 Church of England, Mission and Public Affairs Division: *Response to the House of Lords EU Social Policy and Consumer Affairs sub-committee call for evidence: Inquiry into the EU Commission's Communication on organ donation and transplantation: policy actions at EU level*, October 2007.

and Transplantation Strategic Objectives to 2016/17: Portfolio of Evidence' (2012). These include:

1.21 While the numbers of both living donors (LD) and deceased donors (DD), as well as the number of transplants, have increased markedly since the publication of the Organ Donation Taskforce's report in 2008 and are expected to increase further (DD, 50% by 2012/13, 60% by 2016/17), current practices are unable to meet present and projected demand for organs, with 1,000 individuals dying each year while on the transplant list.

1.22 There are 18.9m people on the Organ Donor Register in the UK (29% of the total population, approximately, 40% of the population over 16). In 2011/12, DD figures were 1088, resulting in 2919 transplants. This represents 37% of eligible Donors after Brain Death (DBD) and 12% of non-contraindicated Donors after Cardiac Death (DCD).

1.23 There is a marked disparity between donor rates and transplant needs among minority ethnic communities, with, for example, members of these communities (11% of the overall population) representing 4% of kidney donors, 22% of recipients and 28% of people on the transplant list. The consent rate among relatives classified in the Evidence Portfolio as 'non-Caucasian' is also low: 27% for DBD compared with 71% for Caucasian relatives; 30% for DCD compared with 54%.

1.24 There has been a sharp decline (15%) in the numbers of deaths of people under 75 years of age in the past decade while there has been a notable increase in donors with a Body Mass Index greater than

30, resulting in fewer average transplants per donor: currently 20% of donors have a BMI greater than 30, compared with 12% a decade ago. 10% of donors are currently over 70 years of age, with an average transplant rate of 2 organs per donor for DBD (compared with 4 per donor for under 50s) and 1.5 organs per donor for DCD (compared with 3 per donor for under 35s).

1.25 Clear difficulties have been identified in the Transplant Pathway. In 2011/12, of those identified as eligible for DBD, 93% were referred to a Specialist Nurse for Organ Donation (SNOD) of which 77% were neurologically tested for DBD. In those tested, 7% failed to lead to an approach being made to relatives, while consent was not given in 36% of cases where it was sought: overall, 37% of eligible donors resulted in transplants. For DCD the referral rate was 54%, the approach rate of those referred was 57% and the consent rate 52%: overall, 12% of non-contraindicated eligible donors resulted in transplants. SNOD involvement in approaching relatives in DBD cases resulted in a 68% consent rate compared with a 53% consent rate where there was no SNOD involvement. For DCD, the rates were 66% and 32% respectively.

Issues Raised by the Consultation

2.1 In addressing a wide range of possible changes to current practices the Consultation raises five issues that have major ethical, social or legal implications:

Change the consent system for organ donation – either to presumed consent for organ donation unless a person has 'opted-out' of the Register, or mandate that people make a choice about whether or not they want to be organ donors (mandated choice);

Targeted engagement programme with Black, Asian and Minority-Ethnic communities and the councils where they live;

Review end of life protocols that conflict with the possibility of organ donation, particularly with regards the early withdrawal of life sustaining treatments in critical care units and emergency departments;

Review the ethical, legal and professional acceptability of so-called elective ventilation (i.e., intubation and ventilation of a gravely ill patient whose death is inevitable in order to promote donation after brainstem death);

Making a person who has signed up to the Organ Donor Register a priority recipient for an organ if they subsequently require a transplant.

The Consent System

3.1 The present 'opt-in' system is based on an understanding that while, in law, bodies are not possessions, individuals enjoy a 'right to use' their bodies while alive and have a right to decide, within limits, what ought to happen to them after they die. Where individuals have not given any instructions with regard to the use or disposal of their bodies after death, next of kin are assumed to take precedence in decision making unless there are overriding factors present, such as a coroner's investigation.

This reflects a careful balance in the relationship between individuals, relatives and the state, with a presumption that the state does not have a right to dictate to either individuals or to their families how their bodies ought to be used. It does, however, accept that there are some exceptional circumstances in which it is appropriate for the state to intervene, specifically where public health might be at risk, where a death might not be from natural causes or where foul play is suspected. The issue raised by the consultation is whether or not the need for more transplants to take place ought to be seen as another 'overriding factor', necessitating state intervention.

3.2 The suggestion that an 'opt-out' system ought to be introduced does not give the state absolute rights over the use of an individual's body. People would still be able to choose not to be donors. It does, however, represent a major, intrusive shift in the state's relationship with its citizens. An overwhelming case would have to be made in its favour before such a shift ought to be introduced and such a case does not, as yet, exist.

3.3 The Transplant Pathway, described in the Portfolio of Evidence, suggests that the most pressing problem in organ transplantation does not lie in getting more names on the Organ Donor Register, but in making more effective use of the nineteen million potential donors already registered. It is clear that much more could be done to narrow the gap between the number of eligible and the number of actual donors, as well as maximizing the number of transplants per donor. More consistent DBD testing, greater DCD referrals and increased SNOD intervention in approaching families for consent ought to have a marked effect in increasing the number of transplants taking place. Similarly, better use of donated organs, utilizing techniques such as liver-splitting and further increases in the use of Living Donors will have a positive effect.

3.4 Greater public awareness and education with regard to the nature of the consent given by individuals signing the Organ Donation Register would also affect the number of transplants taking place. At present, the UK system might best be described as 'soft opt-in', with the wishes of relatives often overriding individual consent. A shift to an effective 'hard opt-in' policy where consent given on the Organ Donor Register is treated in the same way as an Advanced Decision or clause in a Will, would further increase transplant rates. Greater opportunities to consider organ donation by including Organ Donor Registration forms with other forms such as applications for driving or marriage licences is likely to increase the number of people on the Organ Donor Register. At the very least, these and similar interventions aimed at maximizing the number of potential donors ought to be fully implemented before any major change in consent policy is envisaged.

3.5 'Mandated Choice' is a preferable alternative to 'opt-out' in that it recognizes that the state may make requirements of its citizens to provide certain information that is in the public interest (similar to Census or tax returns), while stopping short of implying a prior right to the use of an individual's body. If it were introduced, however, it would be crucial to learn from experience elsewhere which has been problematic. 'Hard Mandated Choice', where individuals must state, 'yes' or 'no' to organ donation has not been successful in jurisdictions, such as Texas, where it has been trialled; it has created resentment, resulting in a high number of people choosing to say 'no'. 'Soft Mandated Choice', where individuals are given the choice of saying, 'yes', 'no' or 'consult my relatives' gives greater choice but still leaves issues to resolve over non-compliance. What penalties ought to be put in place for noncompliance and how would the system be policed? An ineffective law, in this instance, would be highly undesirable, while a new offence and penalties for noncompliance would create a new class of criminal. It has to be asked: is this really a good and necessary way to tackle the un-doubted need to save lives through greater numbers of transplants? Have all other possible approaches been exhausted first?

Minority Ethnic Issues

4.1 It is widely recognized that there are issues specific to minority ethnic communities, although attempts to resolve these issues have not, as yet, been very success-ful. While ethnicity plays a role in finding a matching tissue type in some cases, successful transplants routinely take place between people from differing ethnic groups. Nonetheless the disparity between the number of donors and the number of people on the transplant list from minority ethnic communities ought to be addressed.

In doing so, care must be taken not to dilute or to compromise a foundation principle of the NHS: that treatment is based on clinical need, not on social or economic factors or on a concept of 'merit', a principle affirmed by the Church of England General Synod in February 2012.[2]

4.2 Rather than speak of a *'targeted engagement programme with Black, Asian and Minority-Ethnic communities and the councils where they live'* it is better to consider developing better ways of *partnership working* with representatives of minority ethnic communities and those organizations in which members from minority ethnic communities form a significant part and in which they play a full role. In this context, faith communities have much to offer. The Organ Donation Taskforce and the Organ Donor Campaign have both piloted innovative partnership programmes in recent years that ought to be developed in the future.

End of Life Care

5.1 The General Medical Council's guidelines on End of Life Care place a duty on doctors to act in a patient's

---

2 www.churchofengland.org/our-views/medical-ethics-health-social-care-policy/nhs-reform.aspx.

best interests, while giving weight to patient or family requests for treatment and adhering to valid patient decisions for treatment to be withheld or withdrawn.[3] A review of *'end of life protocols that conflict with the possibility of organ donation, particularly with regards the early withdrawal of life sustaining treatments in critical care units and emergency departments'* would have implications for these principles.

5.2 In the first instance, it ought to be noted that unless a patient has made a valid decision for life sustaining treatment to be withheld or withdrawn, it is incorrect to speak of *'early withdrawal of life sustaining treatments'*. A decision to withdraw treatment is to be made *only* in the patient's best interests and is to be effected at the optimum time in that patient's care; there ought never to be *'early withdrawal of treatment.'*

5.3 That doctors and other healthcare professionals are to act only in what they consider to be a patient's best interests is based on the long-standing principles of beneficence and non-maleficence and is central to End of Life Care. It is essential that these principles are not breached, even in the pursuit of a good cause such as enabling organ donation.

5.4 Where *patient consent* is given for treatment to be prolonged beyond a point where it is *medically* beneficial to him or her, it could be argued that it is in that patient's *overall* best interests to comply with this re-

3 GMC End of Life Care and Advanced Decisions, 'Treatment and care towards the end of life: good practice in decision making', 1 July 2010.

quest because of the beneficial psychological effects it will have. While there are limits to how far this argument can be reasonably sustained, it forms part of the ethical basis for Living Donation. Such operations, which are not without risk, will not benefit donors *medically*, but may be judged to be of overall benefit to them because of the psychological and relational benefits gained in addition to the more obvious benefits offered to the recipient.

5.5 Given the acute nature of serious injuries treated in emergency departments, it is unlikely that it will be possible to gain consent from many patients receiving life sustaining treatments, unless their wishes are already known. Where patient consent cannot be given to pro-long life sustaining treatment after it has ceased to have a beneficial effect it is important that doctors act only in what they perceive to be the *patient's* best interests.

Elective Ventilation

6.1 The issues discussed in a review of End of Life Care are relevant to the practice of elective ventilation. They are made more acute, however, by the fact that elective ventilation represents *actively intrusive* treatment that is not, medically, in the patient's best interests. By its nature, it is unlikely that medical staff will have opportunities to seek patient consent. Elective ventilation was practised in the UK between 1988 and 1994, but was halted by the Department of Health precisely because it breached the 'best interests' principle. In order for elective ventilation to become an acceptable practice, an effective Advanced Decision system would have to be devised. Consideration would also have to be given to its resource implications: as an unintended consequence, other patients requiring ventilation might be denied access to care.

Priority Care for those on the Organ Donor Register

7.1 While this proposal might result in an increase in numbers on the Organ Donor Register, it represents a clear breach of the principle that treatment is given solely on the basis of clinical need and not because of social or economic factors or on the basis of perceived merit. If the merit principle were to be given formal approval for transplant protocols it would be difficult not to employ it in a wide range of other circumstances where lifestyle factors are relevant. Rightly, the merit principle has been formally resisted even if, on occasion, examples exist of it being informally applied.

Church of England – Mission and Public Affairs Council Response to Consultation Document: 'End of Life Care Strategy: Quality Markers and measures for bereavement care and spiritual care at the end of life', 22 July 2011

The Mission and Public Affairs Council of the Church of England is the body responsible for overseeing research and comment on social and political issues on behalf of the Church. The Council comprises a representative group of bishops, clergy and lay people with interest and expertise in the relevant areas, and reports to the General Synod through the Archbishops' Council.

1. We are pleased to have the opportunity to comment on proposed quality markers and measures for bereavement care and spiritual care at the end of life. We welcome the inclusion of these quality markers and measures as an integral and indispensable part of holistic care. Particular attention is given in our submission to the role of chaplains in developing appropriate and effective measures in these sensitive areas as these healthcare professionals are already expert in delivering many relevant aspects of care. Given their expertise in delivering bereavement and spiritual care, it is, therefore, disappointing to note that healthcare chaplains were not specifically included in the list of professions and groups from whom the authors of the consultation document wished to receive responses.

The Introduction

2.1 The stated literature reviews (paragraph 2) are central to the development of quality markers and measures, but we have concerns with regard to the ways in which these reviews have been utilized throughout the consultation document.

2.2 The literature review on Spiritual Care at the End of Life focuses on the roles of three key groups of professionals: nurses, chaplains and social workers. The consultation document, however, does not reflect this in proposing refinements to the existing quality markers. Quality markers can only be delivered through appropriately trained and qualified staff. This requires Trusts to invest in the recruitment, retention and training of key professionals, otherwise there is a danger of devising a paper framework that will be undeliverable in practice. As it is, many chaplaincy departments are currently operating at around fifty percent staffing levels, making it increasingly difficult to deliver adequate spiritual care services.

2.3 The literature review on Bereavement Care highlights problems associated with administrative staff being required to take on non-administrative responsibilities. It pays little attention, however, to the roles that chaplains often play in this area, ensuring that administrators are not asked to act beyond their range of competencies.

2.4 Both the literature review and the consultation document fail to distinguish between grief and bereavement. An understanding of how to deal with grief and, subsequently, bereavement, is part of the role of chaplains, supported by resources within their faith communities. It is questionable if such knowledge is found elsewhere in the NHS, but this point is not recognized in the consultation document.

2.5 Few Trusts are likely to have care pathways in place beyond those dealing with the immediate aftermath of death. Trusts ought to have established networks for the onward referral of those evaluated as having potentially serious post-bereavement support needs. The evaluation of such needs falls readily under the auspices of chaplaincy.

2.6 Reference is made in the consultation document to 'expert working groups' (paragraph 2), but these groups do not appear to have contained any representatives of chaplaincy professional bodies. This may explain the lack of recognition given throughout the document to chaplains as existing expert spiritual care-givers. There may be an underlying assumption behind the document that chaplains only deal with religious spiritual care. In reality this is not the case. Chaplains deal with all aspects of spiritual care both religious and non-religious. Recognition of this fact should be an important part of this document as chaplains already co-ordinate spiritual care in many hospitals, hospices and community settings.

2.7 The professional bodies for Chaplaincy have not been consulted in the drafting of essential parts of this document dealing with such key topics as training, validation and registration of spiritual care givers, standards for work, and ongoing updating of training. This is a surprising omission.

2.8 It is unclear if the development of spiritual care and bereavement markers (paragraph 6) is to be linked to any particular assessment tool for patients and staff. Unless an agreed assessment tool is utilized, there will be difficulties in gathering valid information for auditing patient needs as well as auditing the effectiveness of input and outcomes for patients and staff.

2.9 Historically, commissioners and Trusts have struggled to provide adequate funding for spiritual and bereavement care. With the proposed changes in commissioning via GP-led consortia (paragraph 10) to come into effect over the next few years, measures ought to be put in place to ensure that the delivery of the proposed quality markers is accompanied by adequate funding.

2.10 It is unclear what role, if any, expert spiritual care practitioners (rather than academics) have played in the development of the tailored VOICES version for spiritual care and bereavement (paragraph 11).

2.11 It is regrettable that chaplains are not specifically mentioned in the list of people from whom the authors of the consultation document would like to hear (paragraph 12). Chaplains spend considerably more time providing spiritual care and bereavement care than religious care and they are the main providers of spiritual care within the NHS. It is our conviction that, as appropriately qualified and trained healthcare professionals, chaplains ought to be included as expert or specialist spiritual care givers in this and other related documents. Spiritual Care is a healthcare specialism that can only be delivered safely and effectively by appropriately trained professionals; not by individuals who have only had basic training during a staff induction programme. The consequences of inappropriate spiritual care can be damaging for individuals and their friends and families.

Some key terms used in the debate on assisted suicide

Assisted suicide The intentional act of providing an individual with information, guidance, and/or the means for him or her, voluntarily and intentionally, to terminate his or her own life.

Code for Crown Prosecutors This allows for a degree of discretion on the part of the prosecuting authorities, enabling them not to prosecute if such an action were deemed not to be 'in the public interest'. Detailed guidelines assist prosecutors in coming to a decision whether or not to prosecute, even where there is compelling evidence a crime has been committed.

Involuntary euthanasia The intentional killing of a dependent person for his or her perceived benefit against his or her consent.

Non-voluntary euthanasia The intentional killing of a dependent person for his or her perceived benefit without his or her consent.

Some key terms used in the debate on assisted suicide

Palliative care The active holistic care of individuals with advanced progressive illnesses. It includes management of pain and other symptoms as well as the provision of psychological, social and spiritual support in order to achieve the best experience of life possible for individuals and families.

Physican-assisted suicide The voluntary and intentional termination of one's own life by administration of a lethal substance with the direct or indirect assistance of a physician.

Principle of double effect An action performed to achieve a good and intended effect is permissible even if it also results in an unintended and undesirable effect. An example of this is the administration of necessary pain-relief medication to a patient even if this may have an adverse effect on other aspects of his or her health.

Suicide The voluntary and intentional termination of one's own life.

Voluntary euthanasia The intentional killing of a dependent person for his or her perceived benefit following his or her consent.

Timeline of significant events related to assisted suicide

1984– (NL) The Netherlands Supreme Court approved voluntary euthanasia and physician-assisted suicide under strict conditions.

1992– (USA) California voters defeated Proposition 161, which would have allowed physicians to hasten death by actively administering or prescribing medications for self-administration by suffering, terminally ill patients.

1994– (USA) Oregon Death with Dignity Act passed.

1996– (AUS) The Northern Territory of Australia passed a voluntary euthanasia law. Nine months later the Federal Parliament quashed it. Four deaths took place under this law, all performed by one doctor, Philip Nitschke.

1997– (UK) Parliament rejected by 234 votes to 89 the seventh attempt in 60 years to change the law.

1997– (USA) Supreme Court ruled there is no 'right to die'.

Timeline of significant events related to assisted suicide

2001/2002– (UK) Diane Pretty sought legal protection from prosecution for her husband in the event of his helping her to commit suicide. The High Court, the Law Lords and the European Court of Human Rights rejected her case.

2001– (NL) Voluntary euthanasia and physician-assisted suicide were formally legalized. For 20 years prior to this, PAS had been permitted under guidelines.

2002– (FR) The European Court of Human Rights stated that the European Convention on Human Rights does not include a 'right to die'.

2002– (BEL) Voluntary euthanasia and physician-assisted suicide were formally legalized.

2003– (UK) Parliament rejected the Patient (Assisted Dying) Bill introduced by Lord Joffe.

2008– (LUX) Voluntary euthanasia and physician-assisted suicide were legalized.

2008– (USA) During its first ten years, 341 terminal patients were recorded as having died under the provisions of the Oregon Death with Dignity Act.

2008– (USA) Washington Death with Dignity Act was passed.

2008– (USA) State of Montana legalized physician-assisted suicide.

2010– (UK) England and Wales Director of Public Prosecutions published a 'Policy for Prosecutors in Respect of Cases of Encouraging or Assisting Suicide'.

2012– (UK) Tony Nicklinson and 'Martin' lost their High Court cases, seeking the right to end their lives with medical assistance.

2012– (USA) Massachusetts Death with Dignity ballot measure was defeated.

2013– (USA) Vermont became fourth state to permit physician-assisted suicide.

2013– (UK) The Court of Appeal ruling rejected Paul Lamb's and the Nicklinson family's right-to-die challenges, but granted permission for them to appeal to the Supreme Court.